The Soft Lunacy

Episodes of Literary Obsession

Vincent Francone

Blue Heron Book Works, LLC

Allentown, Pennsylvania

ISBN-10:-0-9991460-6-8
ISBN-13:-978-0-9991460-6-4

Front Cover design by David Schoerner
KarmaKarma Gallery, NYC
KarmaKarma.org
Back cover design by Angie Zambrano

Cover image: with kind permission from the Illinois State Museum
Two Ladders by Gertrude Abercrombie, 1947, Illinois Legacy Collection

Author photo by LO

Blue Heron Book Works, LLC
Allentown, Pennsylvania
www.blueheronbookworks.com

TO MY DOG

Contents

ACKNOWLEDGMENTS

An earlier version of "Poetry Will Save Us" was published by Trish Hopkinson on her blog; "Confession Time" was published, in an edited form, by *The Bosphorus Review*, and a very early version of "My Drinking" was published by *The Tin Lunchbox*.

Excerpts from "The Plunge" and "Last Days at Teddington" from COLLECTED POEMS by Thom Gunn. Copyright © 1994 by Thom Gunn. Reprinted by permission of Farrar, Straus, and Giroux.

Hello

2016 was a bummer. Lots of famous people died, including David Bowie, my musical hero. Trump was elected president, which is baffling. Many of us have spent considerable time trying to figure that one out, though we're not thrilled with the conclusions. The year was grim on the sociopolitical front, but also for me personally. My dog died right after Christmas 2015 and I spent most of the next year mourning him. I had to change apartments. My job started to seem unstable. The media churned out a constant supply of anger and bullshit. Facebook, where I spend far too much time, was confirmed to be the dumb echo chamber we all know it to be, though the steady dopamine drip of "likes" continued to blind us to how out of touch we are with anyone outside our cultivated spheres. Culture seemed on the skids. I read with envy and annoyance the positive reviews heaped on books by edgy poets writing poems about fucking. "Let's fuck the trauma out of each other tonight" and "A zillion ways to fuck" and so forth. Scores of academics got fat grants to write studies of *Star Wars*. My students informed me that making them write a five-page essay was cruel, especially when I only gave them a week to write it. Few of my students bought the books I assigned. Our discussions were limited to talking about the scant info they gleaned from Amazon reviews. I can't blame them. I didn't want to read the books either.

In fact, if there's one thing that 2016 represented to me it was the futility of books. So many were published and yet no one seemed to be reading them. In 2016 I read five separate think pieces on the decline of literacy. Some of these were written by academics arguing against long, deep reading in favor of "educated aliteracy." I'm still not sure what that means. Something to do with being smart enough to get the gist of a book without having to actually read it. In the golden age of television, when Netflix instantly streams first-rate content, who has the inclination to bother with books?

I'm not opposed to passive pursuits. I love movies. There are plenty of great stories to be found on television. I've been reading poetry these last eight months, as I too am finding my need for linear storytelling satisfied by Netflix. Novels have an opportunity to evolve, to become more experimental, to return to the modernist practices that invigorated the 1920s literary culture. And while there are plenty of great experimental novelists writing experimental novels, traditional books with traditional narratives are beginning to seem quaint, antiquated, or—worse—overlong. We've got shit to do. No time for you, David Foster Wallace.

This is bad news for anyone, like me, foolish enough to write books. What's the point? Who'll read them?

But books have long been important to me. I've collected, cherished, and defended them. I'm consistently annoyed by people who say they have no time to read, especially when they also praise the wonders of the internet and the smart phone —"They save me so much time!" One wonders what the hell people are doing with all the time these gadgets save. Probably re-watching *The Walking Dead*.

As seductive as TV can be, I still find myself embracing literacy in an increasingly post-literate world. Normally I'd see this as noble, but 2016 struck me as the time to ask myself why exactly I've spent so much time and money on ink and paper. Why have I kept so many books, even ones I'll likely never read? What the hell is wrong with me?

This investigation into my bibliophilia was inspired by the gloomy feelings that beset me during the first months of 2016. The way to remedy this feeling of melancholy seemed obvious: change your life, Vince. Strip it to the core and examine it. After all, the unexamined life is not worth living. Think I read that line in a book once.

The obvious place to start was the books. They were the focus of so much of my time, money, thoughts, and physical space. And, as the gloom was at its darkest, I no longer saw them as sources of pleasure. They were obligations, burdens, albatrosses around my stupid neck. I'd collected them for what reason? What has driven this obsession?

I see now that the drive to collect books may have to do with their permanence contrasted with the unreliability of people. I know where most of the books in my library are. There's Italo Calvino's *Cosmicomics*. Hello, Kathy Acker's *Blood and Guts in High School*. A good day to you, *Collected Fiction of J. L. Borges*. But where are my old friends? What the hell happened to everyone? Look how quickly that relationship dissolved. Why don't I talk to that guy anymore?

My books are a source of comfort in an uncertain world. The president is an embarrassment, the state of my career is precarious, and people and pets will die off, but that hardback copy of Fernado Pessoa's *The Book of Disquiet* is not going anywhere.

Books, like human beings, are complex and require patience and attention, but, unlike a lot of human beings, they offer stability. Books are difficult. Human beings are incomprehensible.

My aunts like to remind me of all the family gatherings I attended as a teen, events I was required to be a part of, though often I'd find a quiet room and read while my family was downstairs laughing and interacting. Far from shy, I often prefer to be apart from other people. A book is the best way to be alone while staying connected to the savage and beautiful reality of humanity; books give us an understanding of people without having to be among them.

But, of course, this isolation can only last so long. Time to let the eyes adjust to the bright lights of the outside, shake off the dust, and enter the world again. In case things get dull, I'll bring a book.

Tearing Down

January 2016, Chicago, IL

The first days of the year have been shit. In the grip of sadness due to the passing of my cherished dog, and without my wife to grieve with, I have been speaking very little and eating too much. Eggs and potatoes in the morning, pasta for lunch, soup and cornbread for dinner, and lots of snacks between meals. And pizza—I have been eating a steady amount of pizza. All I seem to do is stuff food into my mouth. Food and booze.

Immediately after I dropped Cassandra off at O'Hare airport, I went to the grocery store for supplies, mostly beer and whiskey. I drank the booze in three days, which I've deemed moderate given the circumstances.

Cassandra scheduled the trip to see her relatives in Mexico weeks ago. She was excited about her vacation, but when our dog died only a week before her departure date, the excitement vanished. All she and I have felt since his passing is consuming sadness.

I didn't buy a ticket for Mexico because I planned to stay home and take care of my dog. His heart was bad and he needed pills at specific times throughout the day. Someone had to make sure he got his meds.

I was more than willing to sacrifice time in Mexico, a country I love, to be with my dog. I was aware that he didn't have a lot of time left—the cardiologist told us six to twelve months. He died a week and a half after that prediction.

Our grief has manifested in strange ways, the most significant being that we now hate all our possessions, the furniture, the paintings, even the books. We want to pitch everything and start over, move to a new apartment, maybe a new city, bring nothing with us, shake off the trappings of our lives, all the things we've spent money on that now seem unimportant. Now that I'm here alone, I'm noticing how cluttered the apartment is. *Jesus, look at all this needless shit.*

My wife will return in a week and we'll likely resume some semblance of normalcy, but now I feel oppressed by the amount of crap we've collected over the years.

Why all the goddamn books, Vince?

Why indeed.

At the moment, I'm having a hard time justifying a home library. When I was in my twenties, I moved a lot. Eighteen moves in twenty-two years. There was a lot of couch surfing, a few brief sublets, a squatting situation that didn't last, a short time living with a girlfriend, a long time living with another. The only upside of all this moving is that I managed to keep my possessions to a minimum. But I always had the goddamn books.

I've stopped counting, but if I had to guess I'd say that, at its peak, the library held around 6,000 books. This is a conservative estimation. It doesn't seem like a lot when you're living among them, but when you begin to really look them over, to evaluate each text, the folly of collecting becomes apparent. What the fuck was I thinking? How much time, money, and energy have I spent on these objects? What's the point? It's not like I've read all 6,000. Hardly. And there are some books that I'll likely never read regardless of how long they sit on my shelves. Am I really going to read all of Proust? (I've yet to get past *Swann's Way*.) What about that fat tome of Derrida essays? Or *Being and Nothingness*? And what about the books I've actually read? Why keep them? Do I need to hang onto every Baldwin, Bolaño, and Beckett book? The idea of rereading the writers I cherished in my early twenties—Kerouac, Anne Sexton, Charles

Bukowski, Hemingway—is dreadful. I fear looking at *The Awful Rowing Toward God* with the eyes of a 45-year-old and feeling retroactive embarrassment. And do I need to keep Henry Miller's *The Rosy Crucifixion* trilogy? I mean, there're plenty of places to find jerk-off material outside of those ponderous tomes.

Yet there they are, all the authors and books I adored when I was just starting to understand that reading, and book collecting, is fun. For some time, my identity has been built on the love of literature. Only now do I see that identity as an affectation.

I never liked reading until late in high school. Prior to then, books were oppressive things teachers foisted upon me and that adults read sporadically, though the difference between the school books and the books my mom and aunts read was noticeable. Schoolbooks had dull covers and titles like *The Old Man and the Sea* that sounded pedestrian. There was little to tempt me to look beyond the cover. My mother and my aunts were all very interested in *Flowers in the Attic* and other garish paperbacks. I liked opening the cover and peeking underneath at the secret illustration (a group of scared looking children in a dark room with some specter hovering above them) that clued me in to the creepy contents of the novel.

I asked my teacher what *The Old Man and the Sea* was about. He ran through a rather long speech about the determination of the human spirit and the struggle of man against the natural world. Snooze.

I asked my mother what *Flowers in the Attic* was about. She said, "It's about a very mean mommy." Intriguing, but I still didn't want to read it.

High school, senior year: my English teacher, Mr. Kroc, informed us that we'd be reading a lot of poetry, which, he assured us, was "going to suck." I cringed at first, but somehow he managed to spark my interest in Keats and Shelley. And he got us to read *Brave New World* and *The Razor's Edge* and lot of other texts that I would never have considered. A good teacher, that Mr. Kroc. I'll never forget his assessment of "Ode on a Grecian Urn":

"There's a guy on this vase, and he's got a giant hard-on. And he's chasing a girl with a wet pussy. And they can never get to each other, you know, 'cause they're on this urn. And he's getting harder and harder, and she's getting wetter and wetter, and Keats is trying to say: they're better than we are because they'll never fuck—they'll never satisfy that desire. They'll always just be longing... wanting each other. And you know what? Keats is right."

One of the few advantages of attending Catholic school with no girls in sight was that the teachers talked to us in the most vulgar manner imaginable. As a result, the lessons stuck.

Around that time, I was starting to read between assignments. I was hooked on Stephen King books, horror being my favorite genre. *The Stand* fascinated me; *It* made me lose sleep; *Salem's Lot* freaked me out. I even liked *The Tommyknockers,* not one of King's better efforts. Classmates teased me for carrying fat novels to school, but by then I didn't care. I'd found my group of friends and while none of them were bookish, they were all outcasts at a school that celebrated jocks. My misfit pals welcomed a geek who read horror stories.

I read all of Stephen King and a lot of Dean R. Koontz and some Anne Rice until I tired of those books. So many of the endings were the same. King likes to use fire to erase the evil. Often, people have to simply face the evil and it will go away. It helps if they are children or adults reacquainted with their childhood selves long enough to display innocence and valor. The evil can never win against those qualities.

By the time I got sick of horror fiction, I was enrolled at a community college. I decided to major in English since I liked to read and talk about books, though I regretted this decision when mired in a dull class with a pompous lecturer intent on making me write a report on John Greenleaf Whittier. But the die was cast: I was a bibliophile. I would ride that identity out for the next twenty-five years.

Which brings us to now. Twenty-five years of collecting, reading, thinking and talking about books; taking classes then teaching classes;

writing essays; writing a memoir; writing and publishing some poems and stories; editing poems and stories that probably won't get published; and, of course, moving from apartment to apartment with an ever-growing library. And then, this week, deciding to sell half the books. Maybe more. Maybe less. Maybe I ought to keep this one. You never know. I may want to read it someday and I'll regret having to buy it again. Maybe I ought to keep all twenty-three copies of *The Master and Margarita* I've collected, even the ones in Russian that I can't read. I can be content with only three copies of *Ulysses* and two copies of *Finnegans Wake*, one with my notes and one pristine edition. And how many copies of *The Sound and the Fury* do I have? How many do I need?

See what I'm dealing with?

I've spent many hours going through the library, making piles, lugging boxes and bags around town and making, in four days, a mere $798. Figuring the average price of a paperback, that amount of money would net me only about 50 new books.

I feel utterly foolish. Twenty-five years and what do I have to show for it? A fire hazard in my apartment and $798 in my pocket.

But I'm not done. I've more books to sell before Cassandra gets home. Every night this week I've looked over the books that I'd deemed worthy of keeping, plucked at least five or six titles and moved them to the stack of *to-be-solds*. Then, after further consideration, I've moved some back to the *to-keep* pile. Then sat and looked at the spines piled up in the *maybe-sell* pile and tried to make the hard decision about which to keep, which to lose.

This is too much to do alone. I need an objective partner who will chuck my duplicates and long-ignored texts while I turn the other way and pretend not to know what's happening. At the moment, no such person exists. I have to do this myself. I built the library. I need to be the one to tear it down.

The Bookcase Toboggan

1995, Chicago, IL

Despite the fact that I'd only spent a few months in the apartment, I had to move. My ex-girlfriend, Sophie, left me there. This was supposed to be our love nest, our very first apartment, the one we'd think back on as the place where we started our lives together after so many years of dating while living apart. We'd moved north together from the south suburbs so that we could attend the same university. She was majoring in Spanish and French. I was pretending to be an English major but spent most of my time outside the classroom. I had a low paying job soliciting donations from the university alumni, which didn't afford me much spending money. Sophie liked to spend money. She liked going out to dinner and expected me to come along and chip in on the bill. This was the beginning of our troubles.

After a short time cohabitating, Sophie left me for someone else. That was the smart move on her part.

Only having enough money to live alone for a few months, I asked the landlord if I could sublet the place and get out of my lease. He agreed, though he messed up the date. I told him I wanted out by June 1st. He wrote down May 1st. Subsequently, he found someone to move in earlier than I was prepared to vacate. Which is why I was shocked when a young woman entered my apartment the last Saturday in April. I was naked on the love seat, my bed. She saw me—a hairy, pudgy, hungover slob—sleeping, my legs hanging over the side of the couch. She screamed.

"WHAT ARE YOU DOING HERE?"

9

"THIS IS MY APARTMENT!"
"I'M MOVING IN TODAY!"
"YOU'RE A MONTH EARLY!"
"NO, I'M NOT!"

Eventually the yelling subsided, and we figured out that the landlord had screwed up. We called him and complained, but there wasn't really anything for him to do. This poor woman had hired movers who were on the clock. I had no choice but to pack up and leave.

I placed a few calls. One of my classmates, Carl, agreed to let me crash with him until I could find my own place. The young woman promised me that she'd pay her movers an extra hour so they could deliver my possessions to this new, temporary residence.

"I'll take it out of next month's rent," she said, eager to get even with her new landlord.

The movers got busy moving her things in through the back entrance, but there was no one to help me get my stuff out the front. *I can handle it*, I told myself. I only had some clothes and some books. And a few bookcases.

I'd had these bookcases for three years. My mother took me to Kmart to purchase them. I still have them, though they're barely functional after so many moves. I'm astonished they've survived at all, considering they're made from pressboard. But they were necessary—all those Stephen King books were accumulating on the bedroom floor. But that morning in 1995, lugging them out of the apartment by myself, I was ruing the day I got them. Even flimsy pressboard can get weighty.

The first flight of stairs was difficult, but I managed. When I saw the next flight leading to the entrance of the building, I thought, *Why not?* and placed the bookcase on its back, positioned my ass between two shelves and pushed against the wall behind me. I slid toboggan style down the stairs and through the door, which I'd assumed would break my fall. But the door was no match for the speed and weight of my heft on the makeshift sled. After hitting and opening the door in this most imbecilic manner, the bookcase came to an abrupt halt and I was flung from it to the concrete. Some scrapes and cuts, but no real damage, though a woman pushing a stroller was not amused when I came flying toward her. She said something cruel, but—too consumed with the utter absurdity of my day to address her remarks—I started laughing. This infuriated her further. She left in a huff while I rolled on the concrete, laughing and wanting to cry.

This is just one moving story out of the many I could share, but you get the point: moving books and bookcases is a pain. I'm not looking forward to going through all that again, which is part of the reason I've stayed in my current apartment for close to a decade, despite it being in decline. The bathtub refuses to drain, the roof leaks, there are squirrels and raccoons in the space above my living room—they frequently get in fights, stomping, hissing, and, I imagine, clawing at each other. The air conditioning stopped working two summers ago. My landlord refuses to fix anything, and, thanks to the roof leaks and a slippery set of steps, I took a spill down the back stairs that resulted in an emergency room visit and weeks of physical therapy. Yet I've stayed. Blame the daunting thought of packing and moving the goddamn books, not to mention the bookcases (now fifteen in total). I shouldn't let my personal library keep me rooted in a rapidly deteriorating apartment, but I am. Makes me wonder how the hell I can continue to justify a personal library.

Justifying a Personal Library

January 2016, Chicago, IL

The purge continues. Earlier this week I stacked around 2,000 books in piles on my living room floor. After organizing them into three categories—*keep; to-be-sold; maybe-keep* (meaning: read 10 pages and then consider selling)—I poured a glass of whiskey and sat on the couch. The sight of the books made me angry. Goddamn you, Johannes Gutenberg.

A Gentle Madness, Nicolas A. Basbanes' book about bibliophiles, barely made it back from the *to-be-sold* pile. It seemed right to keep it, me being the gentlest of madmen. Unlike some of the people discussed in Basbanes' book, I haven't traveled the world with the goal of acquiring a single rare book. I haven't married someone specifically to absorb their rare books, though I admit that I changed my reading habits when I moved in with my wife and started reading books reflecting her interests. To be sure, I'm a lesser gentle madman than the individuals detailed in *A Gentle Madness*. My malady is more of a soft lunacy.

My first instinct was to get rid of *A Gentle Madness*. Why keep it? By selling the library I'm proclaiming myself free of books, a bibliophile no more. Of course, by keeping some (a lot, actually) I'm just as sick as ever. The book stays.

What does it mean to be a bibliophile in the year 2016? Aside from the same definition that has always accompanied the term, "A person who collects or has a great love of books," one might add, "A person who ignores the lure of Kindle and maintains that physical books have qualities beyond their contents," or perhaps, "An oddball who thinks it important to be surrounded by dusty tomes." Book collecting is not noble. We soft lunatics may claim otherwise, but we're merely trying to justify our obsession. And what is it about books? Why do we feel so drawn to them?

It must have to do with space. Things that take up space have value over things that do not. A picture of the Arc de Triomphe is nice, but it's no match for the real thing. You can't stand on the picture and gaze out at Paris. You can't feel the bricks, climb the stairs, or truly sense the history from a picture. And while you can certainly read *The Divine Comedy* on a Kindle, holding the tome in your hands, feeling the heft of the thing, adds to the experience. The words are on paper. They are likely to remain on the page. A book on Kindle is illusory. The words come and go. Where do they go? I don't know, but I suspect that the place the words go when they vanish from the backlit screen is not a place that values history, wisdom, or deep contemplation. It's a place that values speed and efficiency, a compact place with a mission to minimize all human thought into something *downloadable*, another word for *disposable*.

Most of my friends have an e-reader of some kind. Many prefer these gadgets to actual books.

"This is the future!" they proclaim, waving their digital device in my face. They champion the e-reader's portability, forgetting that books are also portable, albeit weightier. But the weight matters. The tactile experience is part of the pleasure of reading a book. Running a finger up the spine, rubbing a page between the thumb and index finger, sniffing the pages, caressing them... There's not much onanism to be had with a Kindle.

People who talk of the trees spared by the Kindle are well-meaning and ill-informed.

"I'm being environmentally friendly!" they state, not realizing that electronic devices are at least as, if not more, environmentally damaging as good old paper.

They speak of variety.

"I can tote my entire library with me on the train!" they say, as if that's a good thing. Most of us have difficulty committing to one channel on TV. We scan radio stations while driving, set our Spotify playlists to shuffle and then skip half the songs; we labor over what to eat for lunch, sometimes buying pot stickers from one eatery and falafel from another because, damn it, I deserve to eat whatever I want! If we have an infinite amount of reading material in our laps, how likely is it we'll commit to one book? Books challenge us. They make demands. They're not always easy to follow. They make sophisticated arguments, have knotty plots that require attention, and employ language that sometimes results in a dictionary consultation. Many of us will tire of such challenges and opt for something less involved.

"I definitely want to finish *War and Peace*, but that's enough for today. Right now, I'll settle for the first few pages of Pauly Shore's biography."

When I bring a book from my apartment to wherever I'm going that day, I force myself to commit to that single text. If the language or story or ideas start to make my head do some work, I have no other book to escape to. Yes, I can always pick up my smartphone and read some bit of infotainment, but I'm aware that the book on my lap is the one I chose, the single thing I decided was worthy of sustained focus. Variety is nice, but constant access to anything all the time is a recipe for laziness and distraction. Printed literature is an antidote to a sluggish culture of overstimulation via sensationalistic hogwash.

(By the way, if you're reading this on a Kindle, I take back every critical thing I've stated about e-readers—and I love you very much.)

I make these statements fully aware that there are people with e-readers who can commit to one book at a time. These disciplined individuals have my admiration, but I don't share their self-control. I also suspect that they're the minority. Even if they're not the minority—even if there are still plenty of people reading things longer than tweets and listicles—not all these readers feel compelled to hang onto every book they've read. Reading is often referred to as mental exercise. But weightlifters don't keep every barbell they've touched. So why collect books?

I have no answer that will fully explain the compulsion without making me sound like less of a soft lunatic and more of a truly diseased man. I can argue that, though some of my books have remained unread for over a decade, I can imagine a time when I might get around to them. This sounds crazy even to me, but I have proof that I may someday want to read the micro-fiction of Lydia Davis or Boris Vian or *Appointment in Samarra*.

In 2014, I read *Ulysses*. Prior to then, I'd spent a lot of time actively disliking James Joyce's work. I read *A Portrait of the Artist as a Young Man* in college and declared it overrated. I hated the title (still do). How goddamn pretentious it seemed: the ARTIST as a young man. *La di da!* What a douchebag Joyce was. I didn't understand why a professor once told me that "Araby" is the best short story in the English language. I was far more interested in Virginia Woolf and William Faulkner and, for some reason, thought that adoration of their form of stream of consciousness writing meant that I had to disdain Joyce. And I'd tried to read *Ulysses* before and given up right around the time Stephen Dedalus is wandering the beach lost in his all-important thoughts.

I can't explain why I decided it was time to give Joyce another chance. There's no grand epiphany. I just saw that I still owned a copy of *Ulysses* and decided to try again. And it clicked with me. I suppose when I first attempted to read it, sometime in my twenties, I was too young to really connect with the book. But in 2014, well into my forties, *Ulysses* was waiting for me on my bookshelf. And when I finally finished it, I felt invigorated. What a goddamn great book! I just needed to read it at the proper time. Thankfully, I'd kept a copy.

Having calculated that reading thirteen pages a week of *Finnegans Wake*—the most absurd literary clusterfuck imaginable—would allow me to successfully finish the entire book in one year's time, I began to tackle Joyce's most demanding piece of writing. I finished it in December 2015. I now proclaim *Finnegans Wake* to be a masterpiece, one of the best things I've ever read, a top ten favorite.

I couldn't have predicted that one day I'd read and enjoy Joyce's two most daunting novels. I was hostile to these books even though I sensed that I needed to own copies. I'm glad I kept them. What have I sold this week that I will someday regret parting with?

Fist Fighting Over Bob Dylan

1995, Chicago, IL

My hostility toward Joyce was a result of my old roommates from college, all of them Joyce fans, or at least pretending to be. They liked to drop references to his books, as well as to the works of William Burroughs and Alan Watts, on the coeds who wandered in and out of our dilapidated apartment. Subsequently, I equated Joyce's devotees with a certain type of pretentious college-aged asshole. One roommate, Carl, was the most objectionable person I've ever lived with. In addition to interpreting bohemian life as permission to stop bathing, Carl was a general slob who refused to wash a dish, make his bed, pick up his dirty clothes, or—worst offense—discard his soiled condoms. One morning I woke up, left my bed and stepped on a used prophylactic, lifting my foot just in time to avoid the contents seeping over my bare toes.

When Carl returned home that evening, I asked him to follow me to the bedroom we shared.

"Do you see what I see?" I asked.

"What?"

"That. What the fuck is that?"

"Oh, the rubber... yeah," he said. Then he started laughing.

"Don't laugh! That's fucking disgusting!"

Adequately shamed, Carl disposed of the condom. To his credit, after that confrontation I only saw used condoms on his dresser, not the floor. At least he was no longer leaving his fuck accessories where I might step on them.

My relationship with Carl turned violent one evening during that oppressively hot summer. It was over Bob Dylan. I've never been much of a fan of American folk music, and I especially dislike Dylan's work. Multiple friends have tried to school me in the ways of Robert Zimmerman, and while I might admit that the guy is up to something that resembles important art, it's not for me. If a Dylan song comes on the radio, I'll change the station. If I'm in a bar and someone plays "Rainy Day Women Number Whatever" on the jukebox, I'll grimace through the loutish sing-along about everyone needing to get stoned until a better song comes on. But when I was living with Carl and the other Joyceans, I was subjected to Dylan on a near constant basis. One night the song "A Hard Rain's A-Gonna Fall" was playing and, just after Dylan uttered those words, thunder cracked, and rain fell outside. My roommates cheered.

"Whoa!"

"Dude!"

"Holy shit!"

"That was awesome!"

They were charmed by the happenstance they insisted was Dylan-infused magic. I knew there would be no reprieve from Bob that evening.

The fight was inevitable. I was the sole Dylan hater, the only guy who didn't relish smoking weed and watching *Alphaville* on repeat. The guy who didn't get James Joyce. I was the oddball who didn't seem to be enjoying himself half the time. Tensions were mounting. I pushed it too far one evening by asking if we might have a night off from Bob Dylan. Carl complied by putting on a Neil Young record. I like Neil Young quite a lot, but at that moment I was in no mood to approve of Carl's music choices.

"Great. Another wheezy fuck singing over an acoustic guitar," I said.

"What?"

"At least his harmonica playing is better than Dylan's."

"Vinny, if you don't like it, you can leave."

"Fuck you, take a bath," I said.

Carl pounced.

I've not been in many fights. By no means am I a tough guy, but I was a lot stronger than Carl. I outweighed him, plus he was stoned while I was drunk. That seemed like an advantage. He moved slowly while I moved sloppily, my arms swinging with a sort of boozed-up ferocity. And while he had the element of surprise, I had months of anger behind me. My roommates were getting tired of my grousing, whereas I'd grown to hate them. All their pseudo-intellectual conversations about James Joyce, their inane discussions of the films of Jean Luc Godard, the endless soundtrack of Dylan's "profundities"—I despised all of it, all of them.

We traded a few blows and soon I had Carl pinned to the floor. I proceeded to unload my stored anger on him. I told him that Joyce was overrated, that I was sick of his mess, his stink, his greasy hair and unwashed body. I called Bob Dylan a charlatan.

"You've been duped! You think you're deep because you *love* the lyrics to 'Ballad of a Thin Man'? You think they mean something? Dylan's fucking with you! He wrote that shit in, like, five minutes and you spend your nights analyzing those dumb lyrics like they're T. S. Eliot. You're the sucker!"

I got off Carl and went to bed.

We made up the next day. I apologized for everything I said, and he apologized for jumping me.

"I shouldn't have done that. Not over something dumb like music," he said.

"No problem, man. It's okay."

We never fought again, not even verbally, but we were no longer friends. We did our best to avoid triggering the other, me by staying gone as much as I could. The next summer, Carl went on a vacation to Paris, which he stretched out for months after getting a job as a busboy. His Parisian place of employment was a Chicago themed pizzeria. While living in Chicago, he'd worked as a busboy in a French bistro. Hilarious.

Eventually, the French government kicked him out. He wasn't allowed to work or stay in the country, so he bummed around Europe on his charm, flew to New York, and, once he'd used up most of his money, returned to Chicago. I was living in a new apartment at the time. Carl got my number through mutual friends and called to announce his return. Having developed a distaste for talking on the phone, I let the machine get it.

"Hey Vinny, it's Carl. I'm back in Chicago. I'm throwing a party next week. Call me back and I'll give you the details. Really looking forward to seeing you."

I didn't call him back.

We ran into each other sometime later. He looked good— cleaner than when we roomed together. He told me about a book he'd written while in Paris. Would I look at the manuscript? Why of course.

Paragraph one:

Bulky, unshaven, fiercely came Butch from his basementdwelling, brandishing cigarette and lighter that unconsciously he formed into a holycross with which to bless his morning and all the drudgery of his day, the dishes and the graysoapgrease that floated on the water's surface like pondscum.

I remember this well—I made a copy of this first page and kept it with me for some time, mostly as a means of making myself feel better about my own tendency to emulate my idols. Carl was aping Joyce—the opening of his manuscript is an homage to the start of *Ulysses*. I don't know if Carl realized it or not. Perhaps it was a conscious effort, a Tarantino style shout out to an artistic hero, or maybe he'd immersed himself too deeply in the great Irishman's novel to see that he was ripping it off.

Regardless of his intentions, his book never got off the ground. I find no schadenfreude in this, as Carl made a very fine life for himself. He became a sommelier for a wine bar in Chicago. His job largely consists of traveling the world and tasting wine that the bar may want to import into their cellars. He's supposed to pay for his own lodging while abroad, but he's made more than a few connections in Europe, so he often stays for free while in Austria or Italy. When he's back in town, he gets to hang out at the bar and chat with the sophisticates who frequent the establishment. Pouring wine is somewhat less taxing than working at a busy club or having to deal with the lushes that populate corner taverns. All in all, the guy's done well for himself.

Perhaps I bear some residual issues with my former roomie. So much so that it took over a decade before I could think of reading *Ulysses* and *Finnegans Wake*. In addition to reading two of the greatest works of literature, I've matured. Carl, I've not spoken to you in years, but I hope you're doing well. PS: you were right about James Joyce. Dude was a genius. But Dylan's overrated.

Literary Chicago

Note to agent/publisher:

As you've likely noticed, this book mostly takes place in Chicago. Not being New York or LA, the Chicago setting presents a challenge. It's not a coastal city, so it's not of value; this book is not set in the southwest, so you can't market it as a rugged Sam Shepard-esque exploration of masculinity; it's not set in Mississippi or Georgia (though part of it is in Asheville, NC), so it lacks the southern eccentricity that would give you some kind of angle. It's a tough sell, I know.

Perhaps you can market this book as being a humble addition to Chicago's rich literary tradition, which I assure you is for real. We who reside in this Midwestern metropolis can get a bit boastful when it comes to our writers, as well as our pizza (not just deep dish) and hot dogs sans ketchup. Regardless, many outside Chicago's borders remain unaware of the literary figures this town has produced. To provide context, I offer this brief history of Chicago literature, complete with samples of our finest writers' written works.

P.F.A.

Known only by his (her?) initials, this Chicago born writer (Nov. 15, 1881) got smart sometime after finishing journalism school and moved to New York where (s)he started a satirical column called *The Shifty Skyscraper*, wherein the author's Midwestern tendency toward courtesy was immediately traded in for coastal snobbery, arrogance of the third degree, and "biting" commentaries on all manner of social and political naughtiness. (S)He died on March 23, 1960 of consumption, not having lived long enough to call it tuberculosis.

Sample of P.F.A.:

Is Dorothy Parker a natural raven-hair? From some of the less tight-lipped among her famed Algonquin Round Table, this reporter learned that indeed the runner does match the valances.

Nester Algrish

By far the most renowned of Chicago writers, this novelist was born in Detroit, MI (March 28, 1909) and died in Long Island, NY (May 9, 1981). Between birth and death, Algrish wrote a series of acclaimed books, including *The Man With a Needle Up His Sleeve* and *Stroll Through the South Side*. Famous for playing poker on Ashland Avenue, a stretch of the road has been named in his honor. Each year, local newspapers gather the Chicago literati to award an up-and-coming writer the Algrish Award. Past winners have gone on to be baristas, legal assistants, and bloggers.

Sample:

Frankie Apparatus dealt the cards with a steady hand, the Horse still galloping through his veins. But for how long? Smack has a way of wearing off, and where would that leave Frankie? Shivering in the muscular West Side streets, quivering in neon, a bum steer from a bookie and dead broke. He had to deal off the bottom, get the pot into his pocket if he was going to score a bag of powder from Nifty Jack. It'd be a long night of misery on Division Street otherwise.

Allen Bloomers

Noted academic and author of *The Dumbing Down of America*, Bloomers was born (September 14, 1930) in Indianapolis, IN but moved to the windy city in time to accept a position at the University of Chicago as lecturer. So successful at lecturing, he turned his in-class sermons into a famous interrogation of academic standards in the era of MTV. Convinced that the future of our country's intellectual standing was threatened by relativism, Boy George, and anyone unable to speak Latin properly, he gained notoriety as a champion of cultural standards and an advocate of being born at the age of 40. He died on October 3, 1992 of a heart attack induced by witnessing Sinead O'Connor tear up a picture of Pope John Paul II.

Sample:

When students enter the academy, they are, rightly, to be beset by rigorous prompts, though, in the current university culture, one can hardly find anything more challenging on the average syllabus than Dune. *When asked, most incoming students will brag about not ever reading a book. As concerning as this is, outgoing students, having enjoyed a watered-down curriculum based on the fallacious concept of postmodern relativism, claim their favorite books to be those written by Kurt Vonnegut. It's as if Thackeray or Ayn Rand never existed! Rather than submit to these dangerous trends, it is the responsibility of those in higher education to instill a deep respect for the classics, regardless of their merit. One should not be permitted exit from the Ivory Tower without knowing all of "Paradise Lost" backwards and forwards.*

Ray Brownbread

Along with Ivor Razmataz and Richard Highlands, Brownbread is considered one of the most important science fiction writers in the history of the galaxy. He was born on August 22, 1920 in Waukegan, IL, a part of Chicago not located in the city, though he liked to claim otherwise (this was the beginning of his career as a fabulist). His most enduring works are *Tales From Pluto* and *232 Celsius*, both noted for their imaginative visions of a future that should be here any day now. Brownbread died on June 5, 2012 in Los Angeles, CA, the part of the country where he spent most of his life, it being more conducive to otherworldly speculation than Chicago.

Sample:

Fireman No. 9 set ablaze the cherished Bible of Father McNamara, the latest copy of the good book to be found in this week's purge. It's really something the way they hide these things, thought Fireman 9, you gotta hand it to them. If only they were as dedicated to the State as they were to preserving this crazy old book. Because books are forbidden. And it's my job to burn them. I'm a fireman. Get it?

Gwyneth Rivers

Chicago's most notable poet, Rivers was born in Topeka, KS on June 17, 1917 and moved, by herself, to Chicago at the age of six weeks. Her family joined her shortly after, and the Rivers clan settled in the Bronzeville neighborhood of Chicago, inspiration for many of her works. Rivers wrote extensively about the African-American experience, working-class struggles, feminine oppression, and racial strife and segregation, Chicago being ground zero for each of these topics. Poetry anthologies have honored her by reprinting her best-known poem "Cool We Are" (see below), an easily memorizable poem that has delighted students with its brevity. She died on December 3, 2000 of acute elegance.

Cool We Are

Cool we are, we
So cool, we
Hate school, we
Talk this, we
Can't miss, we
Real sick, we
    Gone quick.

Lara Seisperros

Easily the wealthiest of Chicago born writers, thanks to the success of Seisperros' book *Life on Coconut Avenue*, a text perennially assigned to sixth graders, ensuring constant sales. Seisperros struck gold with this landmark text about a girl growing up in the big city with ambitions to find a better way of life where she can be herself free from the shackles of her family and their old-world ways. The ending has caused debate, specifically when the narrator, Luz, expresses her desire to come back for those she left behind. Chicago based artist and critic Anthony Fitzgerald stated, "Seisperros likens her protagonist's quest to that of the brave boys who fought in Vietnam, many of whom have brothers still waiting for rescue. This is the lamest of false equivalencies." Other reviewers were more forgiving: "Luz's struggle is one that can only be understood by those who've lived as precocious girls battling overprotective immigrant parents. Heteronormative dismissals of Seisperros' work are the death rattle of white boys who fail at creating energetic stories, their own prose devoid of a truly sassy sentence" – Roxy Gray.

Sample:

None needed. You've likely already read Seisperros.

London Fields and Near Death

1999, Somewhere in Iowa

Chris had only been driving for a few months. He was a city kid, born and raised in the Uptown neighborhood of Chicago, which meant that he—having spent most of his life using public transportation—felt no need to get his license. He only took driving lessons after he bought a car, a beautiful Cadillac DeVille that a friend was selling. Chris loved the car so much he bought it without knowing how to operate the thing. I had to go with him to the sale so I could drive the car to his apartment where I parked it and where it stayed until Chris got his license a few weeks later.

Chris named the car Aguirre, "the wrath of god." Aguirre was indeed a sight to behold, and while it was an impractical choice for the streets of Chicago, Chris didn't have it long enough to deal with the lack of parking spaces and narrow side streets. During a road trip, Aguirre died.

"The mechanic even made the sign of the cross over the engine," he said.

Undaunted, Chris bought his second car, a used Dodge Caravan, a more practical follow up to the gorgeous Aguirre. It was in this Dodge Caravan, dubbed Edgar, that I nearly lost my life.

We were speeding down a stretch of highway that ran through Iowa on our way back from Kansas City. We'd spent a good chunk of the previous two days eating shitty food and crashing at a mutual friend's place. At some point we hit a bookstore, and I picked up a copy of *London Fields* by Martin Amis. Chris had recommended the book before and I always ignored his suggestion. But I had no reason to say no when we saw a copy in a Kansas City bookstore. I had *London Fields* with me in the passenger's seat, though I dropped it when we noticed the car wreck to the side of the road. Chris didn't decelerate, even though he was examining the smashed-up cars and not the road ahead. When he moved his eyes back to the road and saw that we were heading toward stopped traffic at 70 miles an hour, he hit the brakes way too hard.

It was quick. We veered from the center lane to the right, somehow managed to avoid the stopped cars ahead and landed in a ditch at the side of the road. Miraculously, Edgar never rolled over. We nearly hit several cars on our trip to the ditch, and one sped past on the left nearly sideswiping us, but our route was unbelievably clean. The only damage was a blown tire. I'm amazed neither of us sustained even a scratch.

Chris didn't have a spare. The previous accident was still occupying the local tow truck drivers, so we had to wait on the side of the road until one of them gave us a lift to a wasteland of dead cars and scattered parts. Chris and I smoked cigarettes, shaking from the adrenaline of near death, while the haggard tow truck driver searched the massive grounds of his junkyard for a tire that would fit Edgar. It seemed likely that we'd be stuck overnight in Middle of Nowhere, Iowa until a Dodge dealership opened to sell us a tire at an inflated cost.

I battled with the cigarette—my first in a year—and tried not to say a word. It would've been easy to add to the stress of the situation by pointing out how close we'd been to becoming road kill, or to chastise Chris for not paying attention to the road, but I kept quiet.

A few minutes before the tow truck driver announced that he'd found a tire for us, I noticed that *London Fields* was under my arm. I remembered dropping it in the van, but I must've picked it up as we exited the vehicle, unconsciously claiming my precious book. Edgar was a death trap. I couldn't leave Martin Amis behind.

After considerable time passed, the tire was on and we were

back on the road. Chris popped a Kinks CD into the stereo and turned "Shangri-La" to ten, and soon both of us were shouting along with the triumphant chorus. We'd made it through a nightmare and were again flying on the highway, heading home with a story now riding along with us, one I would immediately tell my girlfriend, Fern, who waited for me in our apartment.

Her sole response to the story of my near death: "I can't believe you smoked a cigarette."

Go Gentle

Considering the number of individuals I've met in my life, I know relatively few dead people. Most of the people I've met are still alive, though a few seem to be working hard at changing that.

My maternal grandparents passed away before I was old enough to form memories of them, thus I was spared their deaths. I was not so lucky when my father's parents went.

My grandfather's death was quick in the sense that he was active enough to be cooking peppers in his kitchen when he died. This is not to say he was in great shape—he'd endured his time in hospitals and, toward the end, he wore an oxygen tube under his nose (when the mood struck).

Most of us in the family were aware that he had little time left, though it was easy to deny this when the old man was busy making himself a snack or bickering with his wife. Though obviously "in a bad way," he was, thankfully, still in his element.

My grandmother's death was worse. She lingered for quite some time, deteriorating in someone else's house— "hospice" they call it. That seemed like an awful way to go. And though the woman who looked after my grandmother is a saint, and though all of us visited as often as possible, I still felt rotten about the whole thing. At least my grandfather was in his home surrounded by his possessions and the memories of his children and grandchildren playing in those rooms.

Here's the sticky confession: I didn't want my grandmother to die but I really didn't want her to remain alive if doing so meant she'd wallow in such an undignified manner. Admitting as much has made me feel even more rotten than I felt while watching her slip away. I often had the temptation to beat the thought away, to mentally slap it so that it would sink back into the muck from which it rose. But we can never really get rid of these thoughts. If there is a god, it wants us to face our uncomfortable thoughts. If, as I suspect, there is no supreme being, then I can only assume that evolution has insufficiently progressed. We think things that are difficult to speak, things that grant us no peace. Worse, these thoughts are immediately followed by shame. We've not evolved into fully formed creatures equipped to handle all that life will throw at us, not to mention the uncomfortable workings of our own minds. Evolution is not finished. How else to explain the tenacity of troubling thoughts?

Regardless of the shame, I knew that I'd feel better once I got the "Grandma died" phone call.

Lately I've been reacquainted with this guilty feeling. A friend of mine, Ralph, is dying. Ralph was my boss at a used bookshop I worked at in the 1990s. We've stayed close since then, and while I try to visit him as much as possible, the gulf between visits is growing because visiting him is difficult. He's lost a lot of the dignity that we as a species are so concerned with. Functionally paralyzed, he spends his days resting next to a piss jug and at the whims of overworked nurses.

After close to two months of staying away, I went to see him last week. There's always a reason not to visit someone in that condition. Work is constant. I have responsibilities at home. I'm trying to be so many things and being those things takes time. But the truth is I look for reasons not to go because, again, it's hard to see someone when they're so close to the end. When I do visit, I find alongside my dying friend that troubling thought, the sinister elephant in the room: *Wouldn't it be better if he wasn't in this condition? Of course, it would, but that means one of two things—either he gets better, which is impossible, or...* It's the "or" that makes me feel like a monster.

Ralph and I both know that it would be preferable if he were to go to what religious types call "a better place." My friend is in dire condition. He doesn't seem to understand how he's fallen apart so completely. When I came to see him last week, he said little more than "I'm a mess." In the moments when he could focus on a new thought it was along the lines of: "I can't imagine putting up with this for another month." I can't either. How does one tolerate being a bedridden creature that will never see natural light again?

It strikes us both as absurd that his body is so busy clinging to life while it simultaneously courts death. This is a tragicomedy to rival Beckett's best work. In fact, that's how I've often referred to my friend, as Beckettian. And I, dutifully wiping vitamin goo from the side of his mouth and emptying his piss jug, am the dutiful Clov to his immobilized Hamm.

The human body's instinct to fight is almost always celebrated in our culture. We're supposed to battle death as if existence were a boxing match or a war. We fight because to give up is ignoble. Dylan Thomas wrote a poem imploring his father to fight against death. This poem is continually trotted out as a symbol of the indomitable spirit found in the best of us. Rodney Dangerfield's character from *Back to School* summed the poem up this way: "I don't take shit from no one." That goddamn Christopher Nolan movie with Matthew McConaughey used the poem more than once. And while I understand the popularity of the piece—and while I'm glad people are encountering poetry, even if it's spoon fed to them by popular culture—I have to wonder if anyone else has ever wanted to tell a dying loved one to go gentle into that good night.

In a used bookshop this afternoon, I saw a book by Christopher Hitchens: *Mortality*. It was on sale, so I bought it. The book is a collection of columns from *Vanity Fair* that Hitchens wrote after his cancer diagnosis. I read the first thirty pages with surprising joy, considering the subject, and have since been thinking about what it took to compose them. Hitchens was in pain, sick from chemo, besieged by tumors, and the recipient of conflicting messages from friends and foes alike, most of them either stating that they would pray for him even if he, atheist to the end, didn't want them to, or that he was getting his just desserts. One particularly ridiculous message stated that God was punishing Hitchens for blasphemy via throat tumor, the good lord's way of eradicating Hitch's secularist voice. Now there's a dose of Christian love.

The book is sad, to be sure, but even when Hitchens was discussing the terror inflicted upon humanity in the name of God or the fragility of the human body, he could be funny. Gallows humor, I suppose, but how else should one face the unknowable? I've been trying to write about my dying friend in this way, but I can't because I'll never be the writer Christopher Hitchens was. And frankly there's little to laugh about at the moment.

After my last visit with Ralph, perhaps the last I will make, I went to my car and fought tears. Trying to distract myself, I turned on the radio. "Heroes" by David Bowie was on, its grandeur making it both the best and worst song for that moment. I wept. The visit had been awful. Ralph was confused, convinced that it was the middle of the night. When I informed him that it was only 4:30 he asked for confirmation. "4:30, see?" I said showing him the clock.

"PM or AM?"

He then asked what day it was.

"Thursday? Are you sure?"

I was. But he wasn't convinced. And, really, what difference does it make? His days are the same: half paralyzed body, bile-swollen belly on an otherwise gaunt frame, hands that can't hold a book, nurses doing their best, family and friends coming to visit when they can and always looking away when he has to use the piss jug or have his diaper changed (often long after he's soiled it). He distinguishes between Thursday and Friday solely by what's on TV. Sports have been his balm these last years spent in a hospital bed, but even the Cubs' recent post-season activity did little for him. I suppose when one gets to the end, all the things they used to find important seem trivial. Including literature.

I asked Ralph about the book at his bedside, *Wise Blood* by

Flannery O'Connor. He made a noise that conveyed recognition. I sought to end the crushing silence by stating that I haven't read the book but would very much like to someday. He made no sound. Again, what did it matter? Reading literature, like watching sports, is something people do when they're alive. The pursuits, hobbies, and pleasures we devote so much energy to are there to fill the time before we understand how quickly life can crumble. I fear that hearing the eternal Footman advancing will be enough to make any of us realize that such endeavors are meaningless compared to whatever awaits.

When my grandfather died, someone did the requisite job of saying "He's in a better place." At my grandmother's wake, I was informed that she and my grandfather were reunited up above. Fine. I didn't offer any challenge to those claims, but shortly after, while at a family gathering, I heard my brother say that he didn't believe in the afterlife (I have no memory of how that subject came up). One of my aunts was aghast. Did he not think Grandma and Grandpa were together in heaven? He paused, obviously aware that to be honest about his beliefs might seem callus to this woman who'd recently lost her parents. But he stuck to his guns and, as politely as possible, said no, he didn't believe it. I wish I could state that I've displayed similar tact when engaged in theological conversations. I avoid these talks whenever possible, but today I am going to state for the record that I don't really believe the simple answer that others seem so sure of. I can't accept that my grandparents are in a better place or that they are together in heaven. For all I know they are, but it seems unlikely. This is what it means to be an agnostic. You don't know so you don't say anything definitive because saying anything definitive would be egotistical. I mean, who the fuck are you? How the fuck do you know?

I can't believe that my dying friend is heading to a better place. Anywhere is likely to be better than where he is, I suppose, and if I truly believed that he would go to a better place once he died, I'd be less uncomfortable with my thought that it would be better if he passed away soon rather than linger in misery. No, what makes the thought uncomfortable is the suspicion that there is no afterlife, no God, no purpose to existence save for the meaning we assign it. And when you're gone, that's the ballgame. That's why I have such a hard time with my *go gentle* thoughts and maybe that's why we're often so adamant that our loved ones *do not go gentle*—despite proclamations to the contrary, we all know that there is no afterlife, so it becomes important that we rage against death. This is why Dylan Thomas's poem is so enduring. At our core, we recognize the futility of resisting yet know that we may need to hear those words as we're slipping away. Or maybe we'd hear them and realize that they speak to the will of the loved ones surrounding us who can't accept that we're dying, or that they will die, that it will all be over too soon.

There's no way I would ever read the goddamn poem to my dying friend. If I did, he'd probably see it for what it is: a wonderful poem with a selfish message.

The Books You Can't Escape

Some books you can't escape. One of mine is *The Jungle* by Upton Sinclair. I first read this in elementary school, or so I think. Honestly, I can't recall which teacher inflicted *The Jungle* upon me. I just remember thinking it was gross and that meat was disgusting. Of course, I managed to ignore those thoughts long enough to continue eating chilidogs and beef sandwiches for the better part of my youth. The world of *The Jungle* is far in the past. The Union Stockyards closed in 1971, the same year I was born. I used this fact to fool myself into believing that only clean meat has made its way through my digestive system.

Currently, I am using *The Jungle* in one of the college classes I teach, *Writing Social Justice*. The course is supposed to focus on, as the name suggests, social justice issues and the ways writers confront them. My students are writers in the sense that all college students are writers, even if they'd rather not be. It's a required class, one no student looks forward to. They equate social justice with screaming at people, whereas I want them to read some ideas about how systems of oppression have historic precedents and then research some issue that speaks directly to them. Most students are disappointed that I want them to read a book written over 100 years ago. They'd sooner be sharing memes.

Rereading *The Jungle* is a slog. The story is fucking depressing. Poverty, scams, criminality, exploitation, rape, death, and then—worst of all—a sermon on socialism that goes on for far too long. But I kept it on the syllabus partially because it's an example of a book that caused change—Teddy Roosevelt, though he disliked Sinclair, used the book to push the 1906 Meat Inspection Act—but also because I felt that the book was important in and of itself, that the effort of getting through the horrors of 1906 Chicago would benefit my students. I said as much to myself before having to acknowledge that I was doing to them what so many teachers have done to me: insisting on the reading of a lousy book because it's supposed to build character. I've officially become an asshole teacher.

A writer I can't seem to escape is the ever-mythologized Jack Kerouac. I once thought the enduring popularity of Kerouac had something to do with his gorgeous moniker. While I can't stand his books, I must admit that I love saying his name: JACK KER-O-UAC! Such fun.

Today, walking home from a neighborhood bar, I passed one of the free book boxes in my neighborhood, the tiny wooden containers on poles with little doors that, when opened, reveal whatever books area residents have discarded in the name of promoting literacy. The book boxes are called "Community Libraries" or "Little Free Libraries." Some boxes have signs asking me to take a book and leave a book, the suggestion being that I am to feel guilty for not replenishing the little book house. I almost never leave a book.

I've been avoiding them lately. For the most part, I've grown immune to their charms, but when they first began popping up, I would go out of my way to check their contents and snag anything that looked halfway interesting. Soon I realized that the soft lunacy was congealing into a solid, and that if I wanted to avoid bringing extra mildew and dust into my apartment, I'd best curb the obsession. But tonight was different. Blame it on three belts of scotch at the bar, but I had to peek inside. There's only so long one can resist the sirens' song.

The box was mostly empty—just a few old magazines and some children's books—but I did find a copy of Jack Kerouac's *Pomes All Sizes*. A small paperback with a broken spine, it wasn't necessarily an exciting find, but I took it anyway. I haven't read Kerouac in years and really have no desire to read him again. So why take *Pomes All Sizes*? I suppose the soft lunacy can't allow me to pass up a book by anyone so revered as Kerouac. And while I don't give a damn about him or most of the Beats, I was once very fond of *On the Road*. Is it nostalgia that caused me to pick up the book and take it home, where I read a few pages and remembered that—*oh yeah*—I hate Kerouac's poetry?

A few years ago, the original manuscript of *On the Road* came to Chicago. Columbia College had it on display along with a microphone and recording device visitors could use to leave a brief comment. I'm not sure what the comments were supposed to be— praise for the invention of the famous scroll of connected pages that allowed Kerouac to type 100 words a minute without stopping? No one has ever come up with a better comment on Kerouac's process than Truman Capote: "That's not writing, that's typing," but I tried to add something witty of my own. Microphone switched on, I said: "This is a marvelous testament to what little can be accomplished with a lot of Benzedrine."

Kerouac, oh Kerouac. Was I ever so young that I thought his work represented something profound? When did I admire his rambling, embarrassingly self-aggrandizing prose? Was I nineteen? Twenty-one? God, please tell me I was smart enough to see through the bullshit-Buddhism of *The Dharma Bums* by twenty-three.

Though it pains me to admit it now, I was a young Kerouac-off. There was that party I went to where I spent a chunk of time discussing Kerouac with a young woman I was desperate to impress. I'd just read *On the Road* and was pontificating on it like a pretentious asshole. The young woman countered my Kerouac lecture with her analysis of *The Catcher in the Rye*. Between the two of us, the air was thick with neophyte literary talk, so much so that no one else at the party wanted anything to do with us.

It wasn't very long before I started to see Kerouac and his ilk (don't get me started on Gregory Corso) as boring bohemian prigs who couldn't be bothered to stitch together a decent narrative and dismissed the artistry necessary to do so as something worth rebelling against.

Maybe my inability to pass up *Pomes All Sizes* was a product of drunken wistfulness. Maybe I thought I might sell the book to a used bookstore—Kerouac, despite my opinion, is a hot commodity. But I have to contend with the fact that I saw the book and decided, in less than a second, that I had to have it. I'm one step away from trash picking.

It was nostalgia. And the soft lunacy. The two are not mutually exclusive. In fact, nostalgia often drives the soft lunacy. The need to collect, to always be looking for something to add to the collection, is partially based on the idea that once there was a Golden Time. All was grand in that Golden Time. And that time has been lost somehow. This Golden Time can only be regained if one is to fill their current days with the stuff that was around them in that period. If I am no longer the twenty-something Kerouac reading BoHo I once was, then what am I now? Grown up? Responsible? Dull? All of that, yes. And how better to regain some of the pleasures of disaffected youth than by grabbing a book of poems by the very symbol of wayward, quasi-profound hipsterism?

I snagged *Pomes All Sizes* because I wanted to be that person again, the one who once let a fifteen-year-old kid get him drunk.

About that:

1993, Burbank, IL

Rubbing the spine of a recently purchased copy of Kerouac's *Tristessa*, I walked through the doors of the McDonald-Linn Post 541 VFW hall, the gathering place of my grandfather and his cronies and the setting of scores of family parties. My girlfriend, Sophie, followed me in. We'd been arguing a lot that day, mostly because I'd been ignoring her. During lunch, I'd looked over the books I'd bought earlier that day, including *Tristessa*, and hadn't responded to her with much interest. This isn't because I wasn't interested in her. I was too engrossed by the possibility of finding another book that would make me feel as hip and smart as I'd felt when reading *On the Road*. A new continent of possibility had been discovered. I wanted Sophie on that continent with me, but she refused to come along. She hated the obnoxious ultra-cool posturing of Kerouac fans. She loved Agatha Christie books and fantasy fiction. She was writing her own fantasy story, which I'd been subjected to for weeks. It was not to my liking. We didn't share many of the same tastes, so, again, me opting to reread the back-cover blurbs of *Tristessa* during lunch was (rightly) pissing her off.

Sophie was also pissed about having to go to one of my family functions that evening. She was fond of my family, sort of, but she knew what anyone who has ever been around my family learns before long: we're loud and we don't have great listening skills. We talk over each other. We yell not because we're angry but because we're trying to get a word in. We laugh and sneeze and yawn with a level of volume comparable to shotgun blasts. We argue for sport and never take it personally when someone disagrees with us, even if they do so loudly, because we love each other. Outsiders to this chaos tend to run away with headaches and confirmed prejudices about Italians.

At the VFW, Sophie was barely talking to me, so I decided to leave her to her anger and get a drink. Being young and not at all cultured in single malt spirits or fine wines, I opted for the most grown up drink I could think of: I asked the fifteen-year-old kid behind the bar to make me a screwdriver.

Why was there a fifteen-year-old kid behind the bar? I learned from my grandfather that the regular bartender had hurt himself that afternoon.

"He fell off a ladder!" my grandfather said.

The kid, the usual bartender's grandson, was sent to tell the VFW members the sad news. Somehow it was decided that he would make a good substitute for his grandfather.

"What's a screwdriver?" the kid asked me. I told him to just put some ice and vodka and orange juice in a glass. He obeyed, first pouring the vodka until it filled more than half the glass. Then he topped it off with orange juice and, remembering the ice, added a few cubes.

Sweet and sour and poorly balanced, the screwdriver is a bad drink. This wasn't even a screwdriver. Rather, it was a potent dose of vodka with juice to color. I wasn't used to anything that strong, but I drank the quadruple vodka and splash of juice anyway, grimacing at the taste. My head already beginning to swim, I went back to the bar and said, "Kid, make me another like the last." He complied.

Back at the table, Sophie was in the middle of a conversation with one of my aunts. I walked past and found my brother. He told me that our father was remarrying.

"What? He didn't tell me."

"I know," my brother said. "I think he was afraid to say anything about it to you. His exact words: 'Vince is anti-everything.'"

That was a fair assessment. I didn't know what to say to my brother, and my words were already slurring, so I walked away and went looking for Dad. My intention was to confront him, though I wasn't sure why. I wasn't offended by his comment, or by his choice to tell my brother of his impending wedding before me. I was just feeling angry and self-righteous and young and full of booze.

Thankfully, I bumped into a cousin on the dance floor and nearly fell over, making me realize that a sit-down was in order. After a trip back to the bar.

Sophie was free from my aunt and waiting for me. I passed her on my way to the bar, asked the kid to make me another, then returned to my girlfriend.

"You needed a drink that badly?" she asked.

Whatever I said in reply was unintelligible. I gave up trying to communicate and tended to my drink.

"If I ever see you this drunk again, that's it for us," she said. That's about the last thing I remember from the evening. I know Sophie drove me home, because she told me so the next day as she was berating me over the phone. I apologized enough for her to end the conversation, then went back to sleep. Later that day, I read *Tristessa*. It seemed bold and beautiful.

I thought that book was long gone, but it reappeared when I started taking stock of my library and deciding which books ought to go. I don't remember saving it, but there it is on my shelf. Oh Kerouac... you reminder of being immature and stupid, I can't let you go. You keep me grounded, rooted to that callow twenty-two-year-old aspiring bohemian who was anti-everything and convinced that a life of adventure and distinction was inevitable. Oh, to be young again!

The Goddamn Bible

1985-1989, Burbank, IL

During my time at St. Laurence High School, I was forced to study the goddamn Bible. The goddamn Bible was taught as an unambiguous, inflexible text with a fixed meaning that was to be fiercely defended. Priests, nuns, and the Christian Brothers populated my young life, most of them well-meaning in their devotion, all of them unwitting participants in my crisis of faith.

That actually sounds more serious than I mean it to. I hardly had a *crisis of faith*; I simply had to admit that I had no faith at all and that pretending to have any was silly. If there is a God, my phony faith would be an insult to the deity. Anyway, I'm sure that the Supreme Being agrees with me that, out of all the religions created to find a way of understanding God, Catholicism is among the weirdest. And that whole protecting pedophiles thing is impossible for any deity or compassionate human to ignore.

Prior to high school, I was as faithful as your average Catholic boy, inasmuch as I went to church when my family forced me to and forgot about the Father, Son, and Holy Spirit immediately after the communion wafer had dissolved in my mouth, that is when it wasn't sticking to the roof. One is never to chew the transubstantiated flesh of Christ—that would be too much like cannibalism.

I went to a Catholic high school because I hated the idea of going to the same public school as the young men who kicked my ass consistently from grades four through eight. It didn't take long to realize I'd made a mistake—this school was as oppressive as any other, and it swapped girls my age for men in cassocks.

The Christian Brothers were a dying institution. At one point, they made up the bulk of the faculty in the Chicago area's Catholic schools, but during the 1980s the teachers were mostly lay staff, the ones who could have sex without covering it up. The one Christian Brother at St. Laurence who was cool and approachable left the order once his secret girlfriend became pregnant. The worst of the bunch was the librarian, the Brother who was a little too obsessed with our posteriors. I felt his hand on my ass once, though more as a sort of locker room slap than a grope. Regardless, I stayed out of the library after that.

In the 1960s, when my father was a student at St. Laurence, the Brothers were permitted the liberty of beating the shit out of children. My dad has stories of his school days that lead me to conclude that I wouldn't have lasted long under the cruel policy of corporal punishment. This is not to say that a few throwback ass beatings didn't occur. I did see some of my classmates take a smack or two from the older Brothers, the ones who missed the good old days of beating children with impunity. One afternoon, I watched Brother Murray slap the hell out of a kid who had committed the crime of talking back. Swinging his arm and punishing the young face, Brother Murray's eyes positively sparkled.

I never got hit. I was mostly a good kid. At best, I was a C student, but I didn't talk back or screw around in class. Except for a few times. And when I got called out for whispering to a classmate or not following orders, the punishment was always the same: kneel, arms out straight, Bible in each hand. If my arms sagged, I'd hear, "Francone, arms up!" Twenty minutes like that, arms out as straight as I could keep them with the word of GOD weighing on my weak, pubescent muscles. I was fat and soft and the Good Book was teaching me to be strong, to accept my sins and submit to the Holy Gospel. Sweat formed on my head. My heart raced. I wanted nothing more than to collapse. I would've gladly fallen to the floor and howled to God that I was heartily sorry for having offended Thee, and I detest all my sins, because of thy just punishment, but most of all because they offend Thee, my God, who art all good and deserving of all my love. I firmly resolve with the help of thy grace to sin no more and avoid the near occasion of sin. *A-fucking-men!*

Though painful, it didn't take long to get used to the arms out Bible punishment or other ridiculous forms of Catholic discipline. And again, I wasn't regularly given detention (or, as it was called, a JUG, short for "Justice Under God"), but even the few punishments for my slight infractions seemed extreme. It's no wonder I left school with no interest in the so-called word of God.

But I was never without a Bible. I've kept one from high school to this very day. I can't shake the book, just as I can't shake the idea of my own guilt. I'm not entirely sure why I'm guilty or what of, but I know, as do all Catholics, that I'm guilty and need to fall to my knees and ask for forgiveness. And that, apparently, is all I need to do. Ask for forgiveness, sincerely, and I'll be forgiven. Seems so easy, so pure. But I can't. I couldn't ask forgiveness the way they wanted me to, at the end of a proverbial bayonet. *Ask or go to Hell*, I was told. How sincere could my plea for forgiveness be if it was being made under the threat of eternal damnation?

I've not been to church in a long time. Aside from weddings and funerals, I've no plans to return. I did my time with God. He and I are all good. I'll hang onto his book, though. Something to remember him by.

Tracy Williams is a Dirty Girl

Today I bought a used copy of *Jack Straw's Castle and Other Poems* by Thom Gunn, signed by the great poet. I'm thrilled to have a signed copy, but I was less excited when I realized (after plunking down my hard-earned cash) that the book is heavily annotated by its past owner.

Question: What kind of a person annotates an autographed book?

Answer: Tracy Williams of Evanston, Illinois.

Reading a book that someone else has annotated is always interesting. One finds themselves having a conversation with the book's previous owner. In this case, Tracy Williams of Evanston, Illinois, who inscribed her copy of Gunn's poems on February 9, 1978, has a lot to say. Some of her notes belie a woman with a careful eye for literary allusion and a keen sense of what's working in Gunn's work, though I can't help but see something else going on, something that makes me wonder exactly what was on your mind, Tracy my dear.

Take as example this reading of the opening lines of "The Plunge".

Where Gunn writes:

Down of a rope of
bubbles

trapped where you
chose to come

it
is all there is

Tracy has written:

'Where-in I'll trap the conscience of the king.' Heterosexual view of homosexual love. *"It"* = water, sex, the United States.

Oh, Tracy! How'd you get there? "Chose to come" conjured all that? And, really, that's quite a broad assignment of possibilities to the pronoun "it." I'll leave the *Hamlet* reference alone. I'm not the scholar you are, Tracy, so for all I know you're correct in seeing Shakespeare where I see bubbles.

Reading "Last Days at Teddington" through Tracy's eyes was rather interesting. My understanding that the poem is about Gunn's last days in a London suburb was altered when I saw Tracy write "*Sex! Adam and Eve*" next to Gunn's:

So coming back from drinking late
We picked our way below the wall
But in the higher grass, dewed wet,
Stumbled on tricycle and ball.

I imagine there may be something to the "tricycle and ball" that strikes one as dirty. Riding the tricycle might mean... a three-way sex romp? Tripping over the balls? Suppose it's happened to the best of us. Dewy grass is obviously Gunn's slang for moist vagina, right? I won't go into possible interpretations of "coming back" or picking "below the wall."

Oh, Tracy... in 1978 I was all of seven, romping through the dewy grass of my grandparents' backyard while you were all the way up in Evanston reading Gunn. What was happening in your life that caused you to read so much into these poems? Were you so lonely you sought refuge in this slim book, teasing so much from it? Did it get you through that year, the recklessness, the bottled passion ready to burst? Did it heal you after some misspent evenings with other kinky yet skittish suburbanites? And when the year was over, when your ardor cooled and those hot, Shakespearean bubbles burst, did you cast off *Jack Straw's Castle*, no longer in need of the pleasures of its Eden?

Hit it and quit it, eh, Tracy?

No Extroverts

1997, Chicago, IL

The open mics… those wonderful, awkward venues for the unready, unable, untested, and woefully unaware. Every café in Chicago's Lincoln Park neighborhood had a cleverly titled open mic night ("The Odeon" or "Speak Easy" or "Not Chi") where budding poets and musicians and even a few brave standup comedians could play genius. These were forgiving places, tiny coffee houses populated by friends of whomever was going up to share their manic poems or free form trumpet solo, friends who would applaud out of courtesy.

There were no friends at the Discover Café. I had no one to support me as I read my bad T. S. Eliot inspired poems. But I went onstage and read them anyway.

The first poem went over as well as I might have expected had I a shred of self-scrutiny. The poem was a mess. Scattered meter, forced rhyme, references that did little more than demonstrate what I thought to be my erudition—no one cared. I could see it in their faces. But, kind amateurs themselves, they clapped.

The second poem was dirty. I remember suddenly being aware that I was letting the crowd in on more than they may have wanted to know. *Brave, Vince—be brave! You're a POET. You have a VISION. Be true to it!*

The night ended with me running through some poems that I'd scribbled on a page shortly before going up to the mic, work that I thought had some energy and would wow the audience. Of course, the poems were rotten and, worse, I couldn't read my sloppy handwriting and had to ad lib a bit. I'm not so quick on my feet, so the whole event ended not with a bang but a whimper.

I walked back to my table alone, embarrassed and utterly despondent. I was no fucking poet. I had a lot to learn, a lot of terrible poems to write, and a lot more to read before I even knew what poetry was. I watched the next young idiot take the stage and read through some wordplay and mixed metaphors. I felt ill.

Not long after that terrible night, I was at my job ringing up customers at the bookshop. A man walked in. Tall, dressed in a sparkling purple jacket and matching pants and wearing a fedora with an oversized fake feather sticking straight up like a compass pointing north, the man butted in front of a woman waiting to pay for some mystery paperbacks and asked, "Would anyone like to hear a poem?"

"No," answered Ralph.

"You sure? My poems are about hope. And love. Life, they're about life! Who here ain't alive?"

"No thanks," said Ralph. He opened a beer. The woman with the mystery paperbacks looked confused. I rang her up as if nothing unusual was occurring.

The poet wasn't quite done. He dug some photocopied poems out of his pocket and asked if he might leave them, "for anyone who needs to be uplifted by the majesty of words."

Again, Ralph told him no.

"Well then, I will depart but not before wishing you all a most pleasant and blessed evening."

The poet was halfway out the door when Ralph called to him.

"Wait a minute."

"Yes?" said the poet enthusiastically.

Ralph said, "There's never been a good poet who was an extrovert."

The poet smiled and exited the store.

Ralph had no idea what he'd done for me. My failure at the open mic was validated. I wasn't ready to read my poems aloud. I wasn't comfortable up there. Despite being somewhat accustomed to public speaking, I'm always a bit uneasy in front of crowds. I'm not enough of an extrovert to garner attention, which Ralph was essentially saying was okay. No great poet is. I may not have been a great poet, but I wasn't a demonstrably clad goofball pushing his poems on uninterested strangers.

"You really think that?" I asked.

"Uh huh," said Ralph.

"What about Dylan Thomas? Byron? Allen Ginsberg?" asked a customer who'd witnessed the exchange.

"I said 'great poet.' Let me know when you think of one."

Love Affair

I'm not sure why I decided to start collecting different editions of *The Master and Margarita*. It's a great book—one of my favorites—but why hasn't my affection for *Ulysses* and *The Sound and the Fury* and the collected work of Kurt Vonnegut caused me to look for a copy of, say, *Cat's Cradle* while wandering through Mexico City. Instead, upon entering a bookstore in that sprawling metropolis, I went straight for the B section of Fiction and looked for Bulgakov, Mikhail.

At last count, I own 23 copies of *The Master and Margarita*. That's down from 25—I gave a copy to a friend and sold another. Twenty-three seems like a good number—higher than the dull, round 20 and not as high as 30 or 40 or, dear god, 50, numbers that would suggest a worrisome level of mania. No, 23 is a good number for a soft lunatic—high but not outrageous.

I wrote this little essay originally with a detailed description of each copy including publisher, translator, quality of translation, type of book (pocket or trade or cloth-bound), description of cover design, and assessment of readability (font size, page thickness, level of mustiness). I'll not go into all that detail but suffice it to state that there are differences between each copy that make each of them irreplaceable. This is not to say that all are rare editions, not by a stretch, but they're all important, essential.

My first copy is the one I go back to most often. Translation by Diana Burgin and Katherine Tiernan O'Connor, published by Vintage in 1996, paperback trade size, cover: a gorgeous black cat silhouette against a red sky. Plenty of endnotes, should anyone want context, as well as an afterword by Ellendea Proffer. Lots of info, but well-packaged as opposed to the bulkier, more literal but less fun translation by Richard Pevear and Larissa Volokhonsky.

Where was I?

Right, the book. I found my first Bulgakov in a store in the basement of the Sears Tower. I worked nearby and spent a lot of my lunch hours at the bookstore. Aside from having a thing for the young woman who worked there, I liked to browse and read for a bit before heading back to the office. The store employees placed their favorite books on a shelf and wrote cute little paragraphs explaining why exactly their chosen book was recommended. Usually these explanations were long and stated that the book in question was "life changing" and that its prose was "luminous." The employee who recommended *The Master and Margarita* didn't shy away from such hyperbole, though he kept it short: "This is the best novel ever written."

Normally such a claim would elicit an eye-roll, but I was already charmed by the cover design and, despite what they say about not judging a book by its cover, that went a long way. Add the overstatement about it being the single greatest novel and, well, I was intrigued.

I asked the woman behind the counter, the one I had a thing for, if she could second the recommendation.

"Oh, I've not read it," she said and showed me what she was reading, *Ivanhoe* by Sir Walter Scott. That was the day my infatuation ended.

The book... right.

It's fair to say that *The Master and Margarita* is the best novel ever written, depending on your criteria. Saying anything is the best anything ever anything'd is ridiculous, though I might argue that Bulgakov wrote an important, enduring, exciting book that certainly delighted me. I bought that first copy from my no-longer-would-be-paramour and started reading it at the nearby Starbucks, completely losing track of time in the process. Two hours later, I snuck back into the office and avoided the boss for the rest of the day. Two days later, the book was read in full. Two weeks later, I reread it. Two years later, I read it a third time. So maybe it's my pick for greatest novel ever written, but I'm not so sure. There're a lot of great novels that I cherish as well as plenty that are probably measurably better than Bulgakov's, but the book seduced me. It's hard to forget a good seduction.

My urge to find new copies, often in multiple languages, stems from that afternoon in the basement of the Sears Tower. The feeling of happening upon a great book is rare. How often do we wander into a store with no idea what we're looking for and luck into a book that impacts us so deeply? Answer: so rarely that it's enough to get one to believe in some divine force, some hand of fate. Replicating that experience is impossible. I come close to recapturing that feeling when finding copies of *The Master and Margarita* that I didn't know existed. *Look at that cover art! A cat holding a gun! Look at that one! Wow... that one's from the 60s! This one's a hardback!* That's what I'm doing—trying to recreate that afternoon in the basement of the Sears Tower when I stopped having a crush on that clerk and started a longer, more fulfilling affair with a book from the Soviet Union written in the 1930s.

Love Poems from Tom Sullivan

1991, Palos Hills, IL

Tom Sullivan was a hell of a guy. Paunchy and nerdy in a charming, middle-aged man kind of way. With his deep smoker's voice, glasses, thin hair, and slight belly stretching out his wool sweaters, he seemed like the kind of guy who would just as easily get a beer with you as talk about literature. And that's what I loved about Sullivan, that precise combination of erudite poet and working-class regular Joe.

Sullivan taught Intro to Poetry at the junior college I'd landed in after a guidance counselor told me not to apply to a real school. I liked Sullivan immediately. He was funny, approachable, and he seemed a natural extension of the best of my high school English teachers who knew how to make what is often an intimidating subject fun. Michael Donaghy wrote about the way poetry is wrongly taught to young people pointing out that, unlike music, an art form that seems to garner natural appreciation, poetry is forced upon us. We're told that we *must* appreciate this art, that understanding it is *difficult work*, and that only cultured individuals willingly seek it out. This is ridiculous. If one were permitted the luxury of happening upon a good poem or story the way they discover a favorite song, the intimidation inherent in the study of literature might vanish.

Sullivan understood this. He told us on day one that, while he was happy to discuss the techniques that govern formal poetry, he didn't want us to stress about that stuff.

"We're going to read some poems. We're going to talk about

them. We can talk about what we think they mean, or what they *might* mean in addition to what we *think* they mean, but I'm more interested in the way they make us *feel*. Or why we like some and hate others. And you might hate all of them. That's fine. But you'll be expected to tell me why."

Sullivan did the other things teachers do when they want to be popular. He held class outside when the weather got warm. He canceled class when Miles Davis died and invited us to come to his office to listen to *Kind of Blue*. As a break from Byron, he said we could bring in rock lyrics and analyze them as if they were poems. He made jokes during class. He was self-deprecating without devolving into a Woody Allen level of neurosis. He was cultured but had blue-collar roots that he wasn't afraid to let show. He treated us like adults, talked to us like we were real people as opposed to empty heads in need of filling. He didn't take our shit, but he never came off like an authoritarian. He was a perfect teacher.

Of course, there's no such thing. There are only the teachers we need, the ones we find at the right time. That was Sullivan. I needed a guy like him. A role model. Someone who made me think that it was possible to enter the ivory tower. I asked him how he got his job. He showed me the path. It seemed possible: BA, then MA, then find a job at a community college where worries over tenure and publishing and department politics were minimal. I could live in the suburbs and still enjoy the lofty intellectual space where poetry and jazz resided. But they were not so lofty after all. Poetry, jazz, culture, knowledge—they were the stuff of the accessible present, not housed in some far-away castle I would never be let into.

Sullivan assigned a book of poems for each of us to read and write about and asked us to present our ideas to the class as a sort of final exam. When he gave me Anne Sexton's *Love Poems*, I was irked.

"Love poems? Sounds…"

"What? Mushy?"

"Yeah, kinda mushy."

"These aren't those kind of love poems," he said.

And he was right. They were wild, weird, naughty (one is called "The Ballad of the Lonely Masturbator"), morose and sort of creepy (I was a bit grossed out by "In Celebration of My Uterus").

Years later, I would recite the opening lines of "The Kiss" to a girl I was trying to seduce. I had no idea what to say to women but was sure she'd find Sexton's poems as cool and sexy as I did. She did not. She thought they were strange.

"You say that like it's a bad thing," I said, ending the possibility of a second date.

A year after I left the burbs and was pretending to be a student at a big university, I went back to visit Sullivan. He was happy to speak with me, or so he said. Now that I'm a teacher, I know that the space between classes is precious and drop-in visits are not always a treat. But if he felt any annoyance with me, he didn't show it. He asked me how I was doing at the university. I lied.

"It's great," I said.

"What do they have you reading?"

"Right now, Stendhal."

"Heady stuff."

I didn't realize that I was visiting Sullivan to find that excitement again, that same spark I'd gotten from his Intro to Poetry class.

"It's okay," I said. "But I'm not sure I get it."

"From what I remember, you were pretty sharp. You did a good job with Anne Sexton."

"Thanks."

"Hang in there."

None of what he said that day seems especially inspiring, and, come to think of it, none of his lectures were as brilliant as I like to remember. He was probably a good teacher, but I want to think of Sullivan as being bigger than he was. But he was just a good guy who seemed to understand what I was going through, and that's likely what I needed. "Hang in there" was enough. It was perfect.

February 2016, Chicago, IL

12:30 PM. I walk into a room full of eighteen-year-olds who look at me as if I know what I'm doing. I ask them to take out their books and look at page 57. A few of them do as asked; some fumble with laptops and hand-held digital devices. A few do nothing.

"Did you see anything of note in this poem?"

Silence for less than a minute. It feels longer.

"What are the ideas the author is trying to convey?"

Nothing.

"What about the structure. What do the line breaks suggest? Any ideas about the intent of the form?"

Nada.

"Okay, then—how about we just look at a specific stanza. Okay, wait… how about the second?"

Some scanning of stanza two. Some absent stares.

"Alright, the hell with it. Let's start again. Forget about what the poem is supposed to mean or what the poet is supposed to be doing. What did you feel when you read it?"

Zip.

"You did read it, right? I mean, this isn't high school. I don't have to give a quiz, do I?"

A few whispers.

"This is your chance to debunk the theory that your generation can't read anything longer than a tweet."

Laughter.

"Just tell me what the poem did to you. Tell me it did nothing. Tell me it sucks. Tell me anything."

One brave student, Ariel, raises her hand.

"It's lovely, but I have no idea what it means," she says.

"Okay."

"I just don't get it."

"What's to get?"

"Isn't that the point? Aren't we supposed to get some big idea?"

"Tell me your favorite song," I say.

"Huh?"

"Music. You like music, right?"

She names a song I've not heard of. I type the name into the computer at the head of the room and wait for a YouTube clip to pop up. I click on the video and play a bit of the song for the class. Most of them have obviously heard it before. One student sort of sings along but loses the long thread of lyrics that are being spat at the listener.

"What is it about this song that you like?" I ask.

"It's fun."

"What else?"

"The beat," another student answers.

"Perfect. What else?"

"It's cool."

"Wonderful. But what does it mean?"

"I'm not sure," answers Ariel.

"But you like it. You like it not because you completely understand it, but because it makes you react. You can't ignore it. It's interesting. And even if you hated it, you'd feel something, right? You're allowed to have the same reaction to a poem. Ideally, you'll grapple with it and try to find something to say about it, but I'll be happy with 'I just like how it makes me feel when the poet does this' as a response. At least we can build off that. Now reread the poem and pay attention to what it makes you feel. Happy, sad, confused, pissed... whatever."

A few weeks have passed since then. I wish I could say that the students have become lovers of poetry. Some are adding more to the class discussions, though most of them remain unengaged. But Ariel has shown marked interest after that demonstration. I may never inspire Tom Sullivan levels of zeal among my students, and for all I know I was Ariel, the sole student in the room inspired by the teacher's enthusiasm. Maybe I remember Sullivan whipping us all into a frenzy when I was the only inspired student in his class. I'll settle for one student who no longer despises poetry. Small victory, but I'll take it.

Church of the Book

I've started carrying a device with me called a Fitbit. Perhaps you've heard of this gizmo—it's a tiny bit of technology intended to be worn on the wrist, though, because I hate wearing anything resembling a watch, I keep my Fitbit in the tiny pocket above the larger pocket of my jeans. Previously this small pocket served no purpose. Now it's where I house the tracker of my steps. Thank you, Fitbit, for giving this pocket meaning. Its existential crisis has been resolved.

Fitbits are meant to keep one healthy. They may not have been constructed to shame, though that is a side effect of recording the number of steps one takes in a day. I look to my Fitbit app and see that I didn't cross into a five-digit number and feel lousy. Lazy fat bastard. Never mind that I clocked more than 12,000 steps the day before. Today is all that matters. And today I've not properly exercised. How dare I contemplate eating a slice of pizza!

I've become addicted to checking my steps. I look for updates after only an hour has passed. How many steps have I amassed in such a short time? Why did I take the elevator? Just think of how many steps I'd have accumulated had I taken the stairs. And when I do take the stairs, I immediately check to see by how much my number has increased. I'm inevitably let down when 7,206 changes to a mere 7,734.

Yesterday I forgot my Fitbit. A day's worth of steps uncalculated. Deprived that information, I felt lost.

The biggest issue with my Fitbit is that it is old and, thus, faulty. By "old" I mean it has been active for a few years. In the 21st century,

61

any piece of technology old enough to remember a previous presidential election is hopelessly antiquated. In fact, I inherited this Fitbit from my wife when she upgraded to a newer model.

This is also how I got my first smartphone. I would've been content to keep my old flip-phone. It was working fine, despite a few lapses in service and a fragile faceplate, but it made calls and sent texts, which, to me, was all a phone should really do. That a phone could divide its time between being an alarm clock, radio, camera, computer, compass, weather forecaster, boredom killer, and source of constant validation was alien to me. Was I ever so naïve? Oh, to be 45 again!

I mentioned to my wife that her present has begun cheating me of steps. I refresh the app and the number does not change, even after an hour of walking. She reminds me that this is what prompted her to upgrade her Fitbit and that I accepted her used model because, as I must've said at one point, "I don't care if it's old."

"Maybe you should get a new one," she suggested.

I hate the idea of replacing something that hasn't been around long enough to truly be considered obsolete. But that's the era we're in: The Forever New Epoch where everything is made to break.

"For fuck's sake—things are supposed to last. What kind of throw away culture are we living in?" I asked.

My wife is used to these rants, and though she usually cuts me off sooner, today she let me vent a little.

"This is why books are better than any stupid iGadget. Books are made to last. They're only paper and glue, but goddamn it they *endure!* They're portable and strong. You can drop a book and it'll still function, not like an iPhone with its glass face like a fucking baby's fontanel. Books never breakdown or simply stop working. I've got functional books that're decades old."

"Jesus," she said. "Just stop buying anything else, then. Why get your car repaired—it's not a book, so I guess it's not worth fixing? Why upgrade medical technology? All the answers are in books, right? Why not make everything out of books? A house of books.

Better yet, a church—you can just live in there. The religion of books."

She may be onto something. Perhaps I ought to seek out (establish?) a religious order predicated on the belief in the mystery, power, and inherent majesty of the book. I'm not seeking technological regression; I'm no Luddite. But I still wish to preach the superiority of books over digital widgets and doo-dads. In fact, the technological thingamajigs might work best if they are to work in service of the printed page, a technology that—despite a few improvements—has not fundamentally changed much since its invention.

My wife offered a counterpoint: recently we went to Ireland and, while in Dublin, saw the Book of Kells, an ancient illuminated manuscript that is so fragile only one page, under glass, can be viewed per day. I heard that the page turners of the Book of Kells use a pair of tweezers so they won't sully the text with the oils of their fingers.

"So much for the enduring quality of books."

She also pointed out that, unlike books, smartphones and tablets do not get musty and worn. In fact, they have no smell.

"I know—that's why books are better: they have a scent. They're multi-sensual."

"I give up."

Those of us who see the latest iteration of smartphones and yawn are surely going to annoy those around us who champion the never-ending technical upgrades that have rendered so many gadgets obsolete. My TV is too old, not smart, a fossil. My car, a 2011 model, will likely be a relic soon. I suppose I'll fit in well with other prematurely aged grumpy bastards at the bookshops who comb through dusty stacks in search of new ideas packaged in an old and reliable format: printed and bound pages. We'll hold mass between the bookcases, read from Kierkegaard, Joyce, Daniil Kharms. We'll chant the poems of Elizabeth Bishop and Mina Loy. We'll reacquaint ourselves with time and space the way it was understood in the dark

---

ages before Steve Jobs.

I look forward to being high priest of the Church of the Book.

Addiction

1997, Chicago, IL

His name was Kelly. He had a great head of red hair and could swill liquor like a champion. I met him at a party held in my apartment, though I had little to do with planning the soirée, save for being ordered to mix up a batch Purple Passion. My roomies had heard their pal "Piss Drunk Vinny" talk about Purple Passion, a drink made from Grape Crush and Everclear grain liquor. It's a rather silly means of getting drunk, but the roommates thought the drink would go over well.

A few partygoers took sips, but after grimaces and pronouncements that "This shit is lethal," no one was willing to help me drink the Purple Passion. Except for Kelly. I spent a lot of that night slapping the redheaded kid on the back and proclaiming him, along with me, to be the only "real drinker at the fuckin' party." Kelly smiled and laughed and seemed to sincerely love my praise, knocking back more and more of the ghastly concoction until his girlfriend, Anne, told him it was time to go. He could barely stand by that point.

Later that week, Anne called me.

"What the hell is wrong with you?"

"What?"

"Kelly's a recovering heroin user."

"He is?"

"Yes. And now he's drinking every day. Every day since that party where you fed him liquor!"

65

She accused me of cultivating his new dependence on alcohol, of ruining the life he'd been on track toward repairing. I couldn't really argue with her, though I had no idea the kid was battling addiction when I poured Purple Passion down his throat. Still, I felt the need to meet with him and make up for my corrupting influence at the party.

For whatever reason, I brought him a copy of *The Dream Songs* by John Berryman. I thought the poems might appeal to him. Honestly, I don't know what fueled this decision—I think Kelly mentioned something about Sylvia Plath at the party. That he liked, or at least knew of, one "confessional" poet might've been enough to get me to assume Berryman's big collection would be to his taste. Anyway, I felt I owed him something since I'd encouraged his possible alcoholism.

We met at a café. Kelly had stopped drinking for almost 36 hours and was smiling, excited to be sipping coffee in the sunny Chicago afternoon. He seemed genuinely happy to get the book and promised he'd read it and return it and that we'd talk about the poems the next time we got together. I never saw him again.

A few years later, I ran into Anne. I asked her about Kelly, though I really wanted to ask, "What the hell! Where's my book?" She told me Kelly checked into a mental health facility shortly after the day we met for coffee. I can't help thinking that Berryman had something to do with it. Maybe the odd syntax and elegiac poems caused Kelly to snap and decide that life was too big a burden without opiates or alcohol, and that he needed professional help. I don't know for certain—Anne stopped seeing him immediately after he committed himself—but I do know that I lost my Berryman. Maybe it's for the best. Those *Dream Songs* are dangerous.

Notes on a Conference

It's possible that attending conferences can help one get a book published, though book deals are ancillary to the heavy drinking that occurs during, after, and sometimes before the event. There I was among writers, agents, publishers, booksellers, students, interns, volunteers, and janitors, all clamoring for a shot at immortality. Well maybe not the janitors, but, of us, it's likely they had the best stories, though they were too busy cleaning up spilled coffee and discarded sandwiches to share.

The big conference for writers is called AWP, short for the Association of Writers and Writing Programs, a better acronym than AWAWP I suppose. AWP is ground zero for tweed jackets and nose piercings, ambitions and delusions, the talented and the obtuse. I've been to AWP once, an outing that did little more than confirm the ambivalence I feel about my literary dreams.

The conference I recently attended was considerably smaller, a one-day affair designed to be more personal than the behemoth AWP, which really can make a person feel insignificant. All those writers! Each with a manuscript they're dying to add to the mountain of material published each year, most of it ignored. Walking among them, one often feels like a needle in an ocean of needles, all of us pricks.

The night before the event, I joined a typical assortment of conference goers: one publisher, one agent, three writers. Add me, and that makes the equation four writers for every publisher and agent. Seems about right. I was invited to read at a local tavern, an invitation I was happy to accept, though when one of the other writers asked, "Are you really gonna read a *poem*?" I began to rethink things.

The first reader's act was more performance art, funny in an Andy Kaufman/Neil Hamburger way. I laughed, anyway. Next was a translator reading from her English rendering of a Latvian novel. How to follow that? When it was my turn, I shared a short vignette from this very book you're reading. It went over well, emboldening me to try one of my dreaded poems. No one seemed interested in the poem, but I read another anyway. Then time was too short to read another prose piece, which would've likely gone over better. Deflated, I left the stage.

During the post-reading drinking, I was advised to order some meatballs, as the bar is famous, I was told, for the wide variety of sauces they apply to scoops of dead cow. I might've announced to the room that I'm a vegetarian, but I feared this tidbit would be met with as much scorn as my practice of writing poems.

After a lot of drinking and an hour of pinball, I stumbled back to the hotel, nearly getting lost along the way. Getting lost in a strange city is part of the conference experience. Some people will say that it's best to drink at the hotel bar and avoid the possibility of wandering into "the wrong side of town," but those people lack a sense of adventure. Besides, hotel bars are a rip off.

The morning of the conference panels came too soon. A shower, a cup of tea, and a mediocre meal from the hotel breakfast buffet—I was as ready as I'd get to hear industry talks.

The first panel was on editing. Seasoned writers offered useful tips on cutting lines. In tribute to their fine discussion, I'll not add any more to this paragraph.

Next, I had an option: listen to agents talk about query letters or listen to poets talk about their craft. I spent plenty of time in grad school doing the latter, so I went into the room with the agents. This is when all of my worst fears were confirmed. From their conversation I learned that my books are unsellable. One is a collection of short stories. When an unproven writer mentions this to an agent, they will inevitably hear, "Sounds interesting. Do you have a novel?" Another is a collection of poems, which only poetry publishers will give a damn about, though most of the time they won't give a damn. The other is this book, *The Soft Lunacy*, which is hard to describe, even to myself. Not to mention it contains a lot of literary references that will alienate the unfamiliar and may need to be cleared legally for reprint. Adding those obstacles to an already "different" book is sure to keep me unpublished. In fact, I doubt you're reading this.

My dreams dashed, I left the panel discussion oddly optimistic. At least I knew where I stood. Self-publishing panel, here I come!

This panel chat was hosted by four self-published writers, each of them a success inasmuch as one sold a lot of books to people like her who are raising children with special needs, one writes vampire porn, and the others sold enough to get their initial $500 investments back in five short years. This talk was sparsely attended compared to the others with only oddballs like me sitting in the room. Each of us had a book to foist, one that didn't fit in the world of traditional publishing. One of the oddballs asked about length.

"Your book can be as long or as short as you like," answered a panelist, "but audiences do have expectations."

I recognized the oddball from the earlier panel. He'd asked a similar question, informing the agents that, "My novel is around 30,000 words."

"That's pretty short for a novel," one agent said.

"Well, *The Old Man and the Sea* is pretty short."

That the agent didn't reply with "Well, you're not Ernest Hemingway" is a testament to his restraint.

The panels were over. I skipped the chance to pitch my books and went straight to the cash bar. Conference attendees were starting to mix. I found a few familiar faces and tried to chat, though most of the people seemed to know each other and I'm shit at networking. Mostly I talked to a graduate student who aspired to write poetry.

He'd been at the reading the night before and liked my use of rhyme. He asked me some questions about publishing, and I told him what I knew: poems are easier to publish than poetry.

"Huh?"

"There're no end of small, mostly online journals that'll take a chance on whatever individual poems you've got. But a manuscript? Best of luck."

"But there's got to be a better chance of getting poetry published than fiction."

"Sure, and you may not need an agent to get poetry in print. But every time I've published a poem it's been a thrill followed by the feeling that I rushed it. That I'd have done better not publishing it and working on it a bit more. I'm embarrassed by half of what's out there with my name on it. Besides, we're supposed to be writing because we have no other choice, not because we're looking to be the next C. K. Williams."

"Who?"

"Never mind."

Having sufficiently depressed the aspiring poet, I went to my room for an hour of stress eating before heading out to another mixer for more drinking and a half dozen botched attempts at getting an agent or publisher to notice me. Then it was back to the room for a few hours of cable surfing before finally falling asleep.

I regret nothing—I did manage to make a few connections, collect a few business cards, and send a few emails. And I bought eight books at discount, though lugging them on the plane was a chore. Speaking of, the flight home was not without incident. First, a man got ill upon boarding the plane, which delayed our take off. Then, after taxiing for thirty minutes, the captain announced that storms were spotted near Chicago, so the plane was grounded for a few hours. We were advised to leave the plane and wait back in the airport.

O'Hare airport is a hub, and most of the people flying there were connecting to destinations as varied as Denver and Ankara.

Much grumbling and cursing resulted from this delay. I was less annoyed—I was anxious to get home, but that was my final destination. I'd get there sooner or later. I wanted to get away from this tiny airport in this strange city, and from the conference that I'd attended to advance my writing career, but I wasn't worried. My arrival was sure to come soon enough; I just needed to be patient. I wanted to be in a comfortable, ideal place, yet I wasn't opposed to being delayed so long as I knew I was heading in the right direction. My figurative arrival was also delayed, but, despite the dejection of the conference, I was determined. Might take a while, but I'd get there eventually.

On not reading *Infinite Jest*

My bookish friends can be divided into two camps: those who tell me I ought to read *Infinite Jest* and those who tell me not to waste my time.

The ones who say I should read it defend the ambition, erudition, the sheer audacity of the book and make comparisons to other big novels of note like *Ulysses* or *Gravity's Rainbow*. According to his more rabid fans, David Foster Wallace is well within the circle of über-smart writers whose masterpieces exist outside of criticism.

The detractors are often more passionate in their dismissal of Wallace and his big fat book. They speak of it as overly clever, a complaint I understand. I love David Foster Wallace's essays and am sure there's a lot to admire in *Infinite Jest*, but every time I read a bit of it I'm turned off by the cuteness of the thing.

Ralph was not impressed by *Infinite Jest*.

"Maybe someday he'll write something that's not so clever you wanna punch him in the nose."

After Wallace killed himself, Ralph left me a voice mail message: "This is David Foster Wallace calling from the grave. No one here has finished my book either."

I'm thinking of Ralph today, as I got a phone call informing me that he died over the weekend. Quoth Kurt Vonnegut: "So it goes."

Ralph introduced me to a lot of books. It was the one thing we were always able to talk about. During those painful visits to the hospital, when he was bedridden and unable to find comfort, we talked about *Moby-Dick*, "The Emperor of Ice-Cream" (he thought

"Let be be finale of seem" was the best line of poetry written in the 20th century), Faulkner, Woolf, *The Man Without Qualities*... It was a way to avoid talking about how fucked up he was.

I prefer to think back to our last night together at the bar, when Ralph was depressed, having been recently dumped by his girlfriend. In the span of a few weeks he'd lost her, his online business, his meager income, and his apartment. At the time he was living in one of the crumbling transient hotels that used to occupy much of the north side. He spent all day at the Wellington, the bar nearest to his room. The patrons were gruff, "functionally illiterate dodos" who regarded Ralph as a curiosity, a sort of pompous lush who may have had some airs about him but was as rundown and fragile as the rest of them. A day drinker who could recite poetry.

That night, before Ralph was reduced to a horizontal life, we drank beers and talked about books, which further amused the barflies. One of them asked if we were boyfriend and girlfriend. The bartender, a friendly midwestern woman forever clad in a Bears jersey, thought we were weird but liked us enough to consistently buy us rounds. I asked her to make me one of the cheap pizzas in the compact 1,450-watt oven behind the bar, the kind of contraption that burned the pizza and was likely a fire hazard. Ralph ordered a salad and a burger, his usual dinner at the Wellington.

One of the barflies, a youngish man condemned to an electric mobility scooter, approached us.

"Either of you geniuses read this?" he asked, referring to a book on John Kennedy, mostly having to do with his assassination. It looked cheap and dated. I read the back cover, but Ralph wouldn't even look at it.

"Get that away from me."

"What's wrong with this book?" asked the man in scooter.

Ralph just shook his head and attended to his beer. Crestfallen, the guy put his scooter in reverse and backed away.

Ralph closed The Wellington almost every night, but I wasn't inclined to stay until 2:00 AM. My days of late-night boozing were

Vincent Francone

behind me. I saw my nights at the Wellington as a form of checking in on my friend, a duty that I didn't mind, though I wasn't about to put my marriage or my job in jeopardy by staying out past midnight. Ralph understood, but whenever I tried to leave, he'd say, "One more? A quick one?" and I'd either cave, checking the clock behind the bar and measuring what I would say to Cassandra when I got in later than expected, or apologize and insist that it was time for me to head out.

"Work in the morning. Goddamn meeting to go to," I'd say.

"I don't know how you can stand it," he'd say.

"Yeah, it's a grind."

"Teaching those kids. *My gawd!* If it were me, I'd be fired in a week."

"Yeah, I'd love to hear what you'd say to my students."

And then he'd run through a few choice expletives and rant to an imaginary classroom. I'd chuckle and let him try a few other stall tactics, but eventually I'd exit feeling vaguely rotten. Unlike Ralph, I was going home to an apartment that was relatively free of bugs, that had a fair stock of food, that was warm, that had a bed without sweat stains from decades of previous sleepers. I was going home to a dog and a woman who loved me.

February is Chicago's most brutal month. It was on a particularly cruel February night when Ralph stepped out of the Wellington and onto a patch of ice. A slip, a hard fall. Somehow, he got up and limped to his room, though he never made it up the stairs. The next time I saw the guy he was in the hospital. Then he was sent to another for post-op recovery, then to the assisted living facility where he'd spend the remainder of his days.

Now that Ralph is gone, I feel compelled to revisit some of his favorite books. I'm rereading *Moby-Dick* in the morning and reciting "The Emperor of Ice Cream" in my head as I wash dishes. For the hell of it, I looked over *Infinite Jest*. Am I still of the same mind as Ralph? Maybe I've aged enough to appreciate the book and developed the patience to wade through all those goddamn

yz
wv
u
t
s
r
q
p
o
n
m
l
k
j
i
h
g
f
e

footnotes. There are plenty of lit bros who idolize David Foster Wallace and pen their own postmodernist stories and essays and bask in their own cleverness. I'm sure a few of them donned bandanas and stopped shaving and grew their hair long while in college. They likely started playing tennis. Can I see past all their affectations and try to appreciate Wallace's work for what it is, not for the often obnoxious cult that it inspired?

I made it further than I expected. It's ambitious, original, and Wallace's voice remains captivating twenty years after *Infinite Jest* was published. I can see clearly that the author was a genius, a rare mind capable of pulling off 1079-page novel that defies easy categorization. But I can't say I'm inclined to finish the book. Still, I'll keep it. Why not? It makes me think of my grumpy friend and his estimation of the tome, not to mention the advice he once gave me: "If you wanna be a writer, get out of the goddamn English department. Get free of those collegiate fuckers and just write. God help you if you get so steeped in their bullshit you turn into David Foster Wallace!"

Immortal Poems of the English Language, My Little Black Book

In the early 1990s, when I was living in the suburbs and just beginning to form my identity as a literary-minded young man, I found a poetry anthology in a Waldenbooks, the sole outlet for books in the suburbs. These were the days before Barnes & Noble and Borders turned American small towns into places where anyone could find a decent read and mediocre latte.

In this era, Waldenbooks was the only bookshop in town. This worked for me, as I was still mostly reading horror and sci-fi, Waldenbooks' bread and butter (along with steamy romance paperbacks), but soon I was looking for something more. The Waldenbooks in the Chicago Ridge Mall had a slim shelf of poetry, mostly Robert Frost and Carl Sandburg collections with maybe a copy of *The Prophet* for the new age consumer. Among these books I found the pocket paperback of *Immortal Poems of the English Language* that would soon become my most cherished book, though not simply because of the poetry.

I read a lot of the poems, though I was probably more enamored with the book as an idea, this grand collection of the best poetry of the ages, IMMORTAL poems that survived wars, the ends of empires, fiery debate and fickle fashions. These were *the* poems I needed to get under my belt if I was ever going to be a real man of letters.

A lot of the poems were very bad, though I wouldn't admit it at the time. Some of them were, indeed, revered classics and should be read and reread, especially those written by Yeats and Whitman (few women are represented in the book). But the works I first responded to were the sappy love poems, the hyperbolic "Is this the face that launched a thousand ships" speech from Marlowe's *Dr. Faustus*, and the smart-assed poem by Coleridge:

Sir, I admit your general rule,
That every poet is a fool,
But you yourself may serve to show it,
That every fool is not a poet.

While I enjoyed reading the contents, I soon found a new use for the book: I brought it to parties where it made an impression on the young women of suburban Chicago. Most of the men at these gatherings were meatheads in workout clothes who swilled cheap beer and belched between high-fives. Next to them, an awkward kid with curly hair and a Roman nose, covered neck-to-toe in black with a book of poems under his arm, looked quite cool.

This was also the time of *Dead Poets Society*, that terrible movie about an English teacher who shakes up a stuffy school with his radical teaching methods. I thought the movie was exciting, though even then the ending struck me as maudlin crap. But I liked the way poetry was made to seem cool, even a bit dangerous. One lesson from Robin Williams's character stood out—poetry is to be used to woo women. And so, I set out during those suburban weekends to do just that.

It's not like I was the Casanova of the southwest side. I had a few dates, some brief encounters here and there—nothing too serious—but the persona I'd adopted was certainly the source of my minimal success. I attribute it all to that book of poems, my good luck charm. It helped that no female wanted me to read them a poem. They just liked that I had the book with me. This is good— surely, I would've picked the wrong poem or bored them to tears. The illusion is often best.

Looking at the book today: front cover missing, several pages gone. What happened? Why did I neglect to care for this book that was so important to me? Answer: the ex-girlfriend, Fern. She saw the book, thumbed through it and discovered a lot of phone numbers written below women's names, evidence of past flirtations. Jealous and unreasonable, she tore up those pages. It's not that I treasured the information—none of those numbers were likely good anymore, and I was certainly not the one in that relationship prone to cheating—but the fact that she damaged a book was enraging. This was the beginning of our troubles.

But how did we start?

I met Fern when she worked at a cybercafé, which was a thing in the late 1990s, the internet still being something one had to leave the house to access. I worked next to the cybercafé and spent most of my off hours drinking coffee and reading the newspaper while people surfed the net for porn on the sly. I had no desire to get online. It seemed like a chore. These were the days before the world was blanketed in WiFi that guarantees constant connections and endless distraction. Back then one had to log on, which was a pain. I think I may have even predicted, "This internet thing will never catch on."

Fern was tall and chubby with badly dyed hair, a gap between her teeth, and had an awkward way of filling space. But she was flirtatious and genuinely kind when she needed to be. And she seemed to like me. When one of the regular customers would leave the café, having forgotten to log out of their email accounts, Fern would call me over so we could read their emails. One woman, a gorgeous blonde, had an ongoing back-and-forth of dirty exchanges with someone other than her husband. I felt sincerely bad about the invasion of privacy, but Fern calling me over to read these "wet panty emails" was an invitation I was too weak to resist.

Eventually I asked Fern out. I figured I had a shot. My last girlfriend, Sophie, had left me and since then I'd had only a handful of dates, none of them leading anywhere. I was starting to think that the best move would be to get back into a serious, committed relationship and start over, having learned what not to do from my years with Sophie:

1. No more lying about smoking or drinking. If she can't handle my vices, she can't handle me.

2. No more fighting over inconsequential matters. Let her choose a movie, for fuck's sake. So many near screaming matches were started at the video store, Sophie determined to show me her favorite chick flick and me adamantly refusing. Sheesh… compromise, dummy!

3. Don't move in with her. Let the relationship be laid back, take it slow, have fun, don't jump at the chance to play house.

4. Stop trying to get her to like your favorite shit. Yeah, a girlfriend who loves Monty Python, Slayer, and Kurt Vonnegut would be great, but be realistic and don't push your interests on her. Part of being with someone is being with *them*, not the version of them that you wish they'd be.

Of course, all of those rules were quickly broken, especially #1. Fern knew I smoked and drank, but she hated cigarettes and wasn't interested in nights at the bar. She exerted less than subtle pressure and, before long, I was swearing off the coffin nails and pints of Bass Ale. For a few days, that is—I quickly decided that no harm could come from indulging when she wasn't around. I didn't comprehend that cigarette smoke sticks to the clothes and hair, so a fight or two ensued.

Soon we started fighting as if it were the sole means of communicating, not only over my refusal to quit smoking, but about what to watch on TV or what movie to see, or what to have for dinner (bye bye, rule #2). And we were eating dinner together every night because she wouldn't leave my apartment. After our fourth date, I asked her to stay over. How could I have known that she'd take that inch several miles. Before our one-month anniversary, we were cohabitating (so long, rule #3).

I'm not sure what Fern saw in me. We made a poor match.

Perhaps her interest in me was more an interest in my apartment. Her mother had moved from Fern's childhood home to an apartment in West Ridge, a short train ride north, though Fern acted like it was a hundred miles away. She didn't want to move that far from her job, so she just crashed at my place for the next few years.

While I was at work, Fern would watch TV and make a starchy, fatty dinner for us (usually pasta or rice covered in some sort of cheese). When she was at work, I slept in the tiny bed we shared and savored the sprawl space. I'd wake up, smoke on the fire escape, then shower, brush my teeth, rinse my mouth with Listerine, make coffee, drink coffee, smoke another cigarette, eat something, shower and cleanse my mouth again. Then I'd go to work, take a few smoke breaks during the shift, return home and hope that she was out so I could clean up. Usually she wasn't, and we'd fight. Then we'd eat. Then fall asleep on the couch watching *Buffy the Vampire Slayer*.

The night Fern found my copy of *Immortal Poems of the English Language* was not a good one. But it could've been. It could've been the night we broke up. If that would've happened, so much could've been avoided—so many arguments and dull, limp evenings, so many uninspired conversations and bitter compromises, so much resentment. We would've escaped it all. But no—I came home from work and found my proverbial little black book on the pillow of my bed with a note tucked in that read:

I don't know who any of these girls are and I don't care. Call one of these sluts and have her make you dinner. Just don't call me.

When I read the note my immediate reaction was: "Fuck you." But did I say "fuck you"? Well, yes, but I said it to an empty apartment. Did I pick up the phone and call her mother's? Yes, I did. Did I say "Fuck you" when Fern came to the phone? No. I said a bunch of stuff about how she misunderstood, how those were old numbers and old girls in an old book of old poems, that I was with her, that I hadn't done anything wrong, that she'd overreacted.

She hung up.

Well, I thought, *may as well have a cigarette.*

An hour later, she was back. No announcement, she just came over. At that point I wasn't in the mood to see her and had decided that maybe her leaving was for the best. I was on the phone with a friend asking him if he wanted to get a drink when she buzzed the intercom. Shocked, not thinking, I let her up. No real conversation followed; she offered no apology. She just started making dinner in the tiny kitchen. Soon we got to work on the noodles and garlic sauce she'd prepared courtesy of a package of Lipton's instant culinary crime. We shared no words. No fight over my smoking; no condemnation over her snooping. We ate and ignored the tension, watched TV, went to bed, woke up and wasted the next several years.

Notes on Dirty Old Men

1994, Chicago, IL.

I was at a poetry reading. It was not going well. A spate of readers took the stage, all of them running through wordplay and dense images or simple, stripped bare accounts of fucking. Arrogantly, I announced to a friend that I did not wish for my poems to share the same space as those read at the event.

One of the poets, the one who read poems about fucking, approached.

"You reading Hank?" he asked, pointing at the Bukowski book under my arm.

I replied in the affirmative.

"He died, you know."

"What?"

"Dead," he said, then shook his head.

"When?"

"Today."

"Today?"

"Yep. I've been on a bender since I heard the news."

I noticed that he was drinking red wine from a plastic cup. The gallery that was hosting the event was selling it for more than I wanted to spend, but the poet told me that anyone who read a poem got to drink for free.

I took the stage. My poem was bad, but I ran through it anyway, not pausing long enough to consider the reactions it generated. I just wanted it read, and when it was, I stepped off stage as quickly as I could, made my way to bar, grabbed a cup and asked the guardian of the wine, a young woman with pink hair, to "Fill 'er up."

A half hour later, I was drunk. The poet who liked to write poems about fucking was egging me on.

"Bukowski's dead!" he screamed. "What the fuck do you think Hank would've said about this place?!"

"He'd have vomited on the floor, scorned the lack of bravery in this bullshit clip joint."

"Courage! Courage! Where the hell is there any courage, any risk in this place!?"

"That plaster abomination in the corner—you call this art?"

"That splatter of paint over there?"

"Garbage!"

"Empty!"

"Feckless!"

"Cowardly!"

"Where's the wine!?"

We were asked (surprisingly politely) to leave.

The demonstrably masculine posture is one I am familiar with, one I have (in my younger days) consciously adopted, though I never could pull it off. In my twenties, as Kerouac's influence was waning, Bukowski and Hemingway and Céline were waiting to pick up the slack. Theirs was a world-wearier brand of hyper-masculine literature, the sort where the binge drinking and sexual dalliances lead to cynicism. Very appealing to a young idiot trying to keep a few beers down.

For the most part, I've ignored Bukowski out of a need to distance myself from his rather long shadow, though I've defended his work quite often. The most valuable writing instruction has come from his example. Love or hate his work, he produced a staggering amount of writing before his death. He sat at his typewriter, opened a bottle of wine, tuned the radio to a classical music station, and worked for several hours every night. All my educated, opinionated, MFA'd pals who struggle to write three pages a week might learn from his example.

And then there's Pablo Neruda.

Ten years after the death of Bukowski, when I was back in school after a serious lapse in enrollment, I was reading a lot of literature in translation that I felt made me less parochial than I was in my autodidact days. That is, until I was caught reading Neruda.

"Seriously, dude?" said a young woman I'd gotten to know a bit. She was in most of my classes, an English major like me, very interested in things I was just starting to learn about like intersectionality and interculturalism, which, at that time, we called multiculturalism until that term—as I have been recently informed—became taboo for reasons I can't pretend to understand.

"What? You don't like Neruda?" I asked.

"Ugh… where to begin."

"I get it—his poems are sometimes a bit much. Almost purple prose with line breaks, but—"

"No, no. It's his style of cutting women into parts like a fucking slasher. He's the slasher of 20th century poetry."

"Um…"

"Look at this shit." She took the book from me and started to read: "'Body of skin, of moss, of eager and firm milk. Oh the goblets of the breast…' Just listen to this shit! So fixated on the body parts. The tits, the thighs, the 'roses of the pubis.' My god, the fucking *pubis!* How creepy!"

"I think it's supposed to be a celebration of his beloved."

"Well duh! But really, what's going on here—breaking her up into parts. That's all she is to him: thighs, eyes, tits, pussy. Not a woman, no, the '*Body* of a Woman.' That's his concern. Where's her fucking brain in all this? Nowhere. Know why? Because you can't stick your dick in the brain. Ugh… men."

I admit, she had a point. In fact, Neruda might be worse than Bukowski. At least the women in Bukowski's books, though certainly not the characters we're supposed to identify with, are more believable than the impossibly holy and perfect creatures in Neruda's poems. And when Buk got a boner, he called it a boner and didn't try to dress it up as something profound.

Of all of Bukowski's books to let Sophie read, why did I choose *Women*?

"What's this about?" she asked.

"Oh, you know—this guy has a lot of girlfriends and a lot of trouble with them. He drinks a lot. He's kind of a jerk, I guess."

"Then why do you like him?"

I had no answer.

Sophie let out a little "Hmm" then took *Women* with her to the next room. I stayed out of her way for an hour, then told her I was going to the store. She didn't look up from *Women*, just grunted in acknowledgement.

After what seemed a safe amount of time (two hours, long enough to go to the store, buy some groceries, smoke two cigarettes, duck in a convenience store bathroom and rinse my mouth with mouthwash) I returned to the apartment. Sophie was in the kitchen making tea.

"Hey," I said.

"Hello."

"So… you hungry?"

"No. That book made me lose my appetite."

"Seriously?"

"No, not really, but it was pretty ridiculous. This guy, the fat, pock marked asshole gets all these women to sleep with him? I don't buy it. It was nothing more than male wish fulfillment. You all just want pretty women servicing you whenever you like, and you get to be drunk and fat and mean the whole time and these women are supposed to swoon. So stupid."

"So you didn't like it."

"It made me laugh."

"Oh, cool."

"Not that way."

"Oh. Sorry."

"That Hank character—he probably drinks bourbon on the shitter and smells like smoke and stale beer and sweat. Disgusting."

"I suppose."

"I pity the women who fall for these old men playing geniuses. The horrible stink they must endure."

I wasn't sure, but part of me thought she was referring to the smell of cigarettes on my clothes and hair. Was this her way of letting me know that she was aware of my secret habit?

The last time I saw Sophie, she'd just broken up with a guy named Fred Berkhart, a local photographer who, once a week, turned his apartment into a hangout for artists, a sort of salon for the marginally talented hipsters of late 1990s. Fred was in his 60s when Sophie started dating him. He had a long, gray ZZ Top/Walt Whitman beard and always looked one step up from homeless. He wore old, paint-spattered clothing, the kind art students wear to show anyone who sees them that they are, indeed, artists. His breath ran the gamut from sour to putrid. But he was a genius!

"You and Fred, huh?"

"He's a sweet guy, but, you know, the age thing started to get in the way."

"I can see that."

"And he's into some weird stuff. I posed for some photos. Me and, um, another girl. We were just posing—that's all, but it did get a little… weird. Fred never let me see the photos. I think he's got them stashed somewhere along with a bunch of others like that. God—the things he's probably doing with those pictures! Why did I ever agree to pose for him?"

"He's an artist," I said. "I'm sure it was all for his art."

"He's a dirty old man," she said.

"But a genius, right?"

"Sadly, the two are not mutually exclusive."

My Drinking part 1

April 2016, Chicago, IL

A student wants to write her research paper on the correlation between writing and drinking. She's read a bit of Hemingway and—can you believe it?—really likes his work. She's also aware of the infamous drinking done by F. Scott Fitzgerald, William Faulkner, Dorothy Parker, and Malcolm Lowry. I suspect her research will cause her to include John Cheever in her paper, though I'm about to suggest that she scrap the idea and move onto a classic ENG 102 research topic, something like abortion or capital punishment or why marijuana should be legal.

My issue with her proposal: I know that I don't want to read the results. I fear they may scare me. I'll either stop drinking or stop writing, two things I enjoy and do without regard to the consequences.

My drinking has started to be a concern. While my exploits are nothing compared to those of the writers listed above, I'm noticing that lately the bottles are emptying faster than ever. This week I developed heartburn, which Google lead me to conclude was caused by my steady intake of whiskey. I've never had heartburn before, so—thanks to more googling—I naturally assumed I was having a heart attack. After living through the night, I decided to celebrate with a bland breakfast of oatmeal, weak tea, and a banana. *Here's to aging*, I thought. I suppose I would be just fine were I to resume my normal diet of eggs, avocados, tomatoes, and grapefruit juice without the nightly nightcap. But what kind of life would that be?

Were one to examine my words a bit, they might conclude that I'm a drunk. But I'm not a drunk, just a drinker—a fine thing to be so long as the oft-advised "moderation" is practiced. I'm not in denial. I know some real drunks, sad bastards who can't face noon sober. And I love many of them dearly, but I also know that being around them requires a herculean level of patience. I don't think I'm at their level, yet.

Today is April 20th, Hitler's birthday and a date now claimed by marijuana enthusiasts as their holiday. I'm sad that, heartburn still present, I can't have a glass of whiskey (I don't smoke weed, so I celebrate 4/20 in my own fashion). Since I live near a college campus, I usually spend nights indoors with a drink and book, avoiding the clouds of pot smoke hovering over my block. I have nothing against marijuana users, save for the fact that they often stink like a skunk's asshole. But their drug has never been mine. I'm sure these young potheads fancy themselves little John Lennons or Bob Marleys, much the way I thought I was Jim Morrison the first morning I woke up *"and got myself a beer!"*

Beer for breakfast turned to whiskey before bed, both affectations that have become habits. But after this week of heartburn and growing awareness of my mortality, I thought, *Well, maybe it's time to stop.* My drinking hasn't gotten out of hand, but how long until it does? I have friends, older and wiser, who tell me that their drinking caused no end of problems for them, though they were late to show concern for their failing marriages and strained internal—and in one case, external—organs.

"If you keep going the way you do," advised one friend, "you'll be setting yourself up for all sorts of trouble." Of course, this is a friend who likes to invite me over and feed me scotch, which I always have trouble refusing even after draining four glasses. I tried to explain that what he sees is not normal, not my everyday drinking, but try convincing someone that you possess restraint when your speech is slurred.

I'm counting the days since I bought the last bottle and measuring them against the amount of brown liquid left under the label. This is how I evaluate the seriousness of my drinking. That I think of my drinking as a thing called *My Drinking* is a concern—a worry to add to the amount of fat and salt I consume in a day, something I have to lie to doctors about and fret over when the scale tips and the nurse goes *Hmm*. *My Drinking* understands me, though. *My Drinking* whispers and lulls, leads me to bed and tucks me in. And yes, *My Drinking* has a habit of waking me shortly after 3:00 AM when there's no distraction from fears I couldn't face at 10:00. But if I lie in bed panicked for too long, *My Drinking* is waiting to calm me. Name another friend who'll do that for you.

I stopped drinking whiskey in the late 1990s, an era when I ought to have been consistently drunk. Fern didn't drink, and none of my friends wanted to be around me, so I stayed relatively sober. It was an awful time. Fern and I were going through the motions, living together but not really talking, never going out to see a movie or have dinner or go to a concert, just sitting on the couch and watching TV and eating pizza and mozzarella sticks, not a vegetable in sight. Hours would pass without us exchanging a word. One evening, I got up to use the bathroom and didn't close the door. That was a first. I realized it halfway through a piss, but it was too late. I didn't want to bring attention to this, so I said nothing upon returning to my worn out spot on the couch. Fern didn't utter a word about it either. She really didn't care one way or the other. I could perform any necessary, disgusting bodily function in front of her and she wouldn't bat an eye. We were no longer two people sharing an apartment. We'd become one farting, pissing, fried food consuming beast.

Eventually, Fern decided that she was done being part of the monster we'd created, but she wasn't willing to let go of me. She simply wanted to see other people at the same time. I learned this via email. She'd being corresponding with a buddy of mine behind my back. A cyber flirtation, the sort of thing that gave her an out—"It's not like we've actually met in person"—but still angered me. The friend in question, Matt, had turned himself into a bit of internet celebrity. When I'd met him, he was a skinny, awkward comic book nerd, but he transformed into an online hero to basement dwelling geeks everywhere. Fern was a comic book nerd in training. Really, she was just attracted to anyone who displayed a bit of ego, which explains why we originally got together. But living with me had turned her into half of the two-headed couch beast and she, as she put it to Matt, "wanted to remember what it's like to be free."

I wasn't snooping. She sent the email to me by accident. I don't know how; M and V are not that close together on a standard keyboard. Nevertheless, subconsciously or deliberately, she sent the message to my inbox.

When I confronted her that evening, she accused me of reading her private messages. I pointed out that she'd fucked up and sent it to me, but she still insisted I was at fault.

"Why are you flirting with my friends, anyway? Did Matt ever once show you any interest?"

He hadn't. She was simply looking for the next source of validation, which I'd stopped giving her long ago.

We fought inasmuch as there were some nasty words exchanged, but even our fights had long lacked spirit. We were more than done with each other, but too lazy to do anything about it.

I decided it was time to get drunk. Truthfully, I was looking for a reason to go to the bar. It had been too long. This seemed like a good excuse.

During my pre-Fern days, The Red Lion Pub was my second home, the spot for a few pints, glasses of scotch, and heady conversations. I was hoping the bar was still populated by people I used to know. Aside from the bartender, Colin, I didn't recognize a soul. Friends had left town. Some were dead. So, I sat by myself and tried to read the newspaper while drinking. But I couldn't concentrate. The fight with Fern bothered me not so much because she was my girlfriend and I didn't like fighting with her, but because I knew that I was happier by myself in that bar than I'd been in years.

Irked by this revelation, I couldn't even enjoy my night out.

If we were going to break up, I wanted it to be because we were honest about our failing relationship, not because she was pestering my friends via email and looking to date other people. I could handle the idea that we were incompatible, but not that there were other men she wanted to be with. Stupid, stupid ego.

Who cares? You have an out. She's practically cheating on you.

But not really.

Close enough. Get out of there. You'll be free. You can come to the Red Lion whenever you want. No questions about where you've been or how much you've had to drink. No one judging you.

But I made a commitment. I owe it to her to work this out.

Bullshit. You owe her nothing. She took everything from you. Look at you—you fat fuck. All you do is eat shitty food and watch TV. When was the last time you went for a walk? When was the last time you rode a bicycle? When was the last time you had sex? When was the last time you even saw your dick, fat boy?

Alright, alright… but still, I at least owe her a honest break up. I could blame it on her and that stupid email, but that would be shifting all the blame on her. We built this bad relationship together.

Fine. That's very mature of you. But first, how about we hoist a few more glasses?

Why not.

Hoist them we did.

When I got up to leave, Colin the bartender said, "Come back to us when you get tired of married life."

All the time away from drinking caught up with me. I walked home in a deep state of intoxication. It took all I had to find my keys and walk into the apartment. The minute I did, I felt the need to vomit. A quick stumble to the bathroom—*fuck!* The door was closed. I tried it a few times, but it wouldn't budge. So, I kicked it open. Fern was sitting on the toilet. I moved toward her with the urge to be sick, but, seeing her in the nick of time, I turned to the sink and emptied my guts. Fern screamed through this entire episode, which only made me sicker. Her screams, the throbbing in my temples, the queasiness giving way to convulsions, the violent spill of alcohol and bile—it was horrid.

I woke the next morning in bed alone. Fern had gone to her job. She left a note telling me that I'd better have the mess in the bathroom cleaned up before she got home.

Later that night I apologized.

"At least I close the door when I have to piss," was her only comment.

The hangover was fierce enough to send me back to Fern, the two-headed beast reformed. And so, I stopped again—no more booze. *My Drinking* went to sleep for a bit while I sorted my life out. But it was always there, waiting for the next chance to make a scene.

These days, I like to have a customary nightcap that can quickly triple or quadruple if the mood is right. Truth be told, I'm good at saying "when." I don't go overboard unless there's a good reason, though that necessary good reason is easy to manufacture.

Good reasons to drink too much:

Birthdays
Funerals
Births
Good news
Bad news
Break ups
Weddings
A long day of work finished
A long day of work ahead
Stubbed a toe
Ennui
Can't sleep
Need to manufacture bravery
Just watched the news and oh my god
It rained
It's too sunny

Inadequacy

Just won a chess match

Just finished a crossword puzzle

Can't write

Of course, one thinks of the famous line by Hemingway: "I drink to make others more interesting." This is perhaps the best reason I can think of to drink. No wonder bars are open to the public.

Notes on Trash

My father called me an elitist. He said this one Christmas after I announced to the room that I don't care for the film *True Lies*. It's kind of a piece of shit.

"But it's funny," Dad said.

"I didn't laugh much."

"But Jamie Lee Curtis's legs!"

"Well, yeah. Those are pretty great, but did I need to endure Tom Arnold just to see those legs? I'd sooner watch *A Fish Called Wanda* if I want to marvel at the sex appeal of Jamie Lee Curtis."

"You're a film snob."

"Me?"

"Elitist."

I informed my family that I love horror films, grindcore metal, and that I have a soft spot for the movie *Cinema Paradiso*—a schmaltzy, sentimental thing engineered to get me to cry and hate myself for doing so. How can I be an art snob when I love a lot of the stuff considered junk by true elitists?

The accusation of elitism has also come after I made the grave error of telling some fellow college instructors that I don't really care about *Star Wars* films, video games, or the Marvel Cinematic Universe. Pop culture is now the stuff of academic discourse, dissertation papers, and classroom lectures. Those of us who enjoy a lot of pop culture but don't need a bloated scholarly text to justify Batman movies are starting to be seen as weirdo traditionalists. How dare I make my students read Jonathan Swift when there are so many great zombie books I could assign?

The problem is, Swift is a dead white male, and, as such, his work does not mesh with the current political culture that (rightly!) seeks to promote works by underrepresented groups. I'm not making a joke about this—women, ethnic and racial minorities, and those whose sexuality does not adhere to heteronormative tradition have largely been excluded from the canon. While I don't debate this and see every reason to pay attention to ignored voices, I'm not about to ditch *all* the dead white men. And if I do, it will be for the work of Jeanette Winterson, Virgilio Piñera, Anna Akhmatova, Marina Tsvetaeva, Orly Castel-Bloom, Aglaja Veteranyi, Helen DeWitt, Jean Toomer, Kathy Acker, G. Cabrera Infante, Reinaldo Arenas, Medbh McGuckian, Nuala Ní Dhomhnaill, Ana Castillo, Manuel Puig, Ralph Ellison, Jessie Fauset, Leontia Flynn, Clarice Lispector, or Elisabeth Bishop. All of these remarkable writers have produced challenging, engaging, and astounding works of literature that should be read, discussed, and reread. All of these writers are, in my allegedly elitist view, worthier of university attention than a lot of the potboilers and vampire stories currently generating praise.

This is not to say that a potboiler or vampire story is inherently bad or even lesser than so-called literary work. But I do see the importance of assigning texts that ask students to grapple with ideas and see possibilities beyond those offered by popular culture. Few of us need prodding to watch a superhero movie or read a genre novel. But now that classrooms and dissertations are full of deep thinking about seemingly shallow works of art, the mere suggestion that one ought to read something denser than a Young Adult novel is met with the "elitist!" indictment.

I'm tempted to blame Susan Sontag's *Notes on Camp* for starting the trend of finding artistic value in what was once easily dismissed as sensationalistic fun. I've only read this essay once, so forgive me if my memory of it proves faulty. I could reread it in preparation for this essay but, frankly, the idea of doing so irks me. I don't want to grant Sontag's ideas on camp the respect of reconsideration. Not because she was wrong or that the essay is crap or that camp is a bad thing, none of which is true, but because I'm tired of camp, trash, and kitsch.

Even the horror films I used to go through like Kleenex are beginning to repel me.

My wife and I have had many dates centered on leaving the house and paying hard earned money to watch enigmatic psychos eviscerate gorgeous young people. Every Halloween—when the local theaters screen "classic" horror films—we spend hours in uncomfortable chairs, our feet stuck to dried cola and popcorn grease, all in the name of camp. But I'm at the age where such forms of entertainment, however giddy they once made me, seem crass and stupid. Witnessing CGI bloodbaths and lame-brained ghost stories is a tolerable means of whittling away an evening, and some of these movies do still manage to shock in ways that feel inventive, but more often than not I feel cheap after letting these films do to me what I knew they were going to do: shock, titillate, and mindlessly amuse. I've let them have their way with me and, even if I sort of enjoyed the experience, I inevitably feel worse about myself after. The post-movie trip back to the car is like a morning walk of shame.

The first time I felt genuinely rotten after sitting through a film was when a friend and I went to the midnight showing of *Caligula*, the notorious 1979 porno posing as historical romp. We sat front row center and watched the fucking, fisting, and beheadings. What fun! Until it wasn't. During the first twenty minutes, the entire audience laughed at the vulgar film. An hour in, some tittering was heard. By the ninety-minute mark, no one was amused. My friend had reached his limit. "Let's bail," he said. I protested—we'd paid money to see the movie. We should finish it. His response: "I'll pay you to leave with me now."

I was resistant to leaving because enduring the repulsive movie seemed necessary, as if by doing so I could better measure something within me. Who I am is who I am in response to *Caligula*. And at the age of twenty-two I wanted to be a person who found trash fun, who knew about B cinema and defended it with intellectual flair. But I was full of shit. I was just into the sex and gore and the sheer audacity of it all. It was a middle finger to elitism. There was no way for me to realize just how elitist I was being by insisting that we stay to finish *Caligula*, how I was asking my friend to join me in the small group of select individuals who were ready to call this astonishingly bad film "art."

Caligula, for the record, is so bad it barely qualifies as trash. It features Peter O'Toole, John Gielgud, Malcolm McDowell, and Helen Mirren, top-notch actors, though they barely elevate the shit-show. A movie that is similarly repugnant and admired is *Salò, or the 120 Days of Sodom*, the 1975 Pasolini film my cinephile friends tell me is important. They defend the movie by insisting it's about the sickness of the fascists or the depravity of art or something, but I find the film simultaneously dull and gross. Better in some ways than *Caligula* but still nasty and not as shocking as *Cannibal Holocaust*, a movie that is at least honest in its sick, exploitive nature. No script by Gore Vidal, no highly respected actors struggling to justify their participation, no shit eating masked as political statement—just ugly people doing ugly things for an ugly audience.

I used to think the purpose of trash was to offer a distinguishing element allowing one to see the difference between it and art. Now it's all mixed up and supposedly equally worthwhile. Goddamn postmodernist cultural mash-ups! And again, I still do enjoy some of the trashier stuff, and I have no problem watching costume-clad heroes beating up computer-generated monsters, but I've never really been one for writing a thesis paper on any of that shit. Superhero movies and slasher films are more enjoyable without a theory behind them.

How do we separate trash from art? I have my way of determining which is which, and I'm not so pompous as to insist that anyone adopt my views, though I've gotten into some debates over the years, often in classrooms. A student recently tried to convince me that video games are the novels of the 21ˢᵗ century.

"This is how we experience narratives. Why read a book when you can shape the narrative? Games let you do that. Books will be obsolete soon."

If I hear this bullshit one more time I'll smack someone on the head with a copy of *Anna Karenina*.

Books are going nowhere. Movies and television have not killed the book. I doubt that Call of Duty poses any greater threat. And while I'm willing to admit that video games are likely valid and culturally significant, I just don't give a fuck about them. When people tell me that I should try to play this game or that one, that I will lose myself in the experience, I immediately think, *Well, isn't that what I'm already doing when I read a good book?*

I suppose my real concern is that the lure and accessibility of popular culture is supplanting material that requires greater effort and attention. There's nothing wrong with entertainment that provides immediate stimulation, but great art makes demands on us. Important demands. When we reject the challenge of art—when we fill our lives with sit-coms and reject more nuanced or complex fare—we sacrifice the pleasures of cultivation. When we have not worked to digest the complex story or idea, when we've solely fed on simple carbs and sugars, we become momentarily full but not nourished. Stuffed, but not fed. There's plenty of room for pie and ice cream, but maybe some vegetables and lean proteins first?

Even as a student I found myself fighting for what I called a balanced artistic diet. A very good teacher once said, "Some days we want the intellectual equivalent of filet mignon and some days we just want intellectual White Castles." A diet too rich in White Castle sliders would surely result in gastro-intestinal damage; best to make such an indulgence a rarity and get in the habit of eating something green and natural. Similarly, an Adam Sandler movie never hurt anyone (save for the casual racism and sexism) but a cinematic diet of nothing but Happy Madison productions may be hazardous to one's intellectual health. Reading pop novels may not be a bad pursuit, though I assume *Twilight* books should be balanced with something a bit more redeeming. Then again, reading this lighter lit—which Jeanette Winterson called "printed television"—is still reading, and in a culture where Twitter may be the most popular form of writing, any form of sustained reading should be celebrated. Or not. I mean, if we agree with Winterson then surely there are important, difficult texts and frivolous, emptier books. What's the result of conflating all books as being equally important?

The answer may be what I experienced while earning my BA. I was enrolled in a class called American Women Writers. Along with some very good material by Willa Cather, Toni Morrison, Nella Larsen and Carson McCullers, the class was assigned *Odd Girl Out* by Ann Bannon. I didn't like the book. I understood its importance, but it felt like badly written pulp. Fun, sexy, cool, and maybe worth reading in a historicist context, but not as good as "The Ballad of the Sad Café" goddamnit.

As my classmates went on about the merits of Bannon's story, I held my tongue. The book was being celebrated as a feminist classic—smut written by a woman that presented lesbianism less as a thing to titillate men than as an honest, legitimate form of romantic love. And I was all for that, but I couldn't overlook the lousy syntax and dreadful dialogue. And I knew that was merely my reaction, one I wanted to keep to myself, but after the professor pressed me to chime in on the discussion, I decided to share my thoughts.

"It's just not my thing."

"Not everything is written for you!" exclaimed a classmate. By "me" she meant a straight white male.

"I know, and I'm not saying that everything has to be for me, but I don't have to like everything either, right? I mean, I like what the book did, you know, historically, but not the book itself, if that makes sense?"

"Can you be more specific?" asked the professor.

"Well—the writing kinda sucks. Just my opinion, but it's badly written. It was a struggle to get through it. Maybe I was spoiled by having just come off Carson McCullers, you know, 'cause her writing is so good—it's just difficult to downshift like that."

My views were deemed elitist.

"You can't say that one book is better than another," said a classmate. "It's subjective."

"Okay," I said. "But, well, the writing… it's just not good. I'm judging it on its, you know, formal qualities, not the content."

"*Formal qualities?* That's the very definition of elitist! You insist that a book adhere to your prescribed notions of 'good' when this book, this brave novel from a brave woman, is more raw and real than the overly decorous prose you favor."

That the phrase "overly decorous" would never have popped up in Ann Bannon's book seemed lost on my fellow student. Other words and phrases she bandied about that semester that would also not have appeared anywhere in Bannon:

Post-modernity

Intersectional

Obfuscation

Calumny

There's something odd going on when big words are applied to works full of small ones. It's almost as is if one must use the big words to prop up the work comprised of small words in order to show how the work with small words is really a BIG work, not the small one you may think, but no, something BIG and IMPORTANT despite appearing small and trite. The struggle to elevate pulp, camp, or even obvious trash to the level of great art seems ridiculous. It's a lot more fun if you just take it for what it is and don't strain to spin straw into gold. Don't put truffle oil on Domino's pizza. *Repo Man* and *Big Trouble in Little China* are immense fun. I'm not going to dress them up as anything more. One of the joys of so-called guilty pleasures is that they need not be defended. Stop trying so hard—just enjoy your trash.

How Not To Travel to Lisbon

2008, London, Paris, Lisbon

One might think that a book collector like me would spend his time in London looking for texts by, I don't know, Kingsley Amis or Philip Larkin or some other quintessentially British writer, but I was thrilled to find several G. Cabrera Infante novels. Specifically, *Infante's Inferno*, a hefty tome I opted to carry with me through the rest of my European trip, it coming in handy during a nightmare excursion from Paris to Lisbon.

My fellow travelers: Chris, who nearly killed me in his van while driving through Iowa; my Cassandra, who almost always knows what will happen before I do; and D.C, an oddball from Virginia who'd moved to London to forge a new life.

As a group, we weren't in stride, having hit some rocky patches in Paris when D.C., a bona fide Francophile, decided to leave the apartment we rented to go adventuring on his own. We felt a little abandoned, though Cassandra and I had each other's company. I suspect Chris felt like a third wheel as we boarded a tour bus and saw the sights.

After a few days, Chris and D.C. reestablished their bond and went off to do their thing while Cassandra and I walked through Paris on our own. The night before we were to leave the City of Lights, Cassandra decided that not walking down the Avenue des Champs-Élysées was absurd.

"We need to walk down that street."

And we did. After days of unnecessary trips on the stinking

Metro, not to mention meandering to find the allegedly hip spots that the locals frequent, Cassandra and I realized that the apartment we'd been sleeping in was ridiculously close to the Louvre and the Champs-Élysées. We spent an evening walking that magical street until we reached the Arc de Triomphe. 284 steps up a stairway and we were on top of the Arc looking down at the city, which, goddamnit, was gorgeous. All these years I'd been resistant to seeing Paris. I always remembered the way Carl would describe the city in ways that seemed too hyperbolic to be real. I'd wanted nothing to do with Paris, but that night changed my mind. I was in such a good mood that whatever tensions had started developing between us and the rest of our group seemed silly. We were friends. There was no reason to bicker.

The next evening, we left Paris and headed to Lisbon, which was tops on my list of places to visit. I'd been listening to Fado music and reading the Portuguese writers Fernando Pessoa and António Lobo Antunes in preparation. D.C. had booked us passage on a train from France to Portugal that ran from 11:00 PM to the next morning. We figured we'd sleep on the train and wake in Lisbon refreshed and ready for breakfast.

"We have a six-berth car, so there'll be two other people in there with us, but we'll be fine," he said.

It sounded okay to me. I imagined the scene from *Some Like It Hot* where Jack Lemon is surrounded by scantily clad women eager to share drinks.

Immediately upon seeing the accommodations, we knew we were fucked. The train car was tiny and the beds, stacked in threes on either side, were too thin for the sort of sleeping that allows for serious rest. And the other two passengers were a married couple as miserable as any I've ever met. The woman was amiable enough, especially after Cassandra managed a fractured conversation with her in a mix of French and Spanish, but her husband—rotund, hairy, decked out in sweat pants and suspenders—was a ghastly sight. He barked a command at his wife who, without a word and in mid-conversation with Cassandra, rolled onto her back and closed her eyes. The rest of us moved to the food car for coffee and tense conversation. Chris, visibly upset, proclaimed that D.C. had wasted our money. D.C. became defensive. I tried to make a joke, but no one had found me funny for days. Cassandra sat quietly, the smartest of us for not opening her mouth and making things worse.

Somewhere in all of this squabbling we decided that it was only one night, that we could, if we had to, stay up until we got to Lisbon, then crash for a bit and go out for dinner. Plan B was to find an empty car and hide there, which we did, each of us sleeping while sitting up. This worked well enough until a ticket-taker asked for our passes.

"This is not your car," he said after looking at our tickets.

"We don't like our car," D.C. said.

The man was unsympathetic. Cassandra tried some French on him. It worked somewhat; he decided that two of us could stay if we agreed not to take up more than one seat (the other was reserved). The other two would have to return to the tight six-birth car with the fat man and his put-upon wife.

After an awkward pause, Cassandra announced that she and I would go back to our assigned car. I don't remember if Chris and D.C. thanked us. I want to write that they did because I want to avoid making them out to be assholes, especially Chris who I still love, though I know that we weren't on great terms at that moment. Truth: I have no memory of any "Thank you." And I hated them at that moment, cursing their names as I opened the door to our sleeper car and heard the loudest, phlegmiest snores ever produced by a human being.

Cassandra took the top bunk and I took the one under her, eye level to the fat man, as I discovered when he woke up and decided to stare at me. I tried to ask him if he was okay, but he just stood there in the dark looking me directly in the eye, his face inches from mine. His sewer breath erupted in a belch. He then scratched himself and went back to his bunk. I could hear him moving beneath me. Sleep proved impossible. I feared closing my eyes and inviting the fat fuck to do as he pleased with my resting body. And I had to protect Cassandra. This guy was strange, repulsive, and clearly abusive to his poor wife. Maybe he had designs on us? No, sleep was not an option.

What felt like an hour passed. After more monstrous snores, the fat bastard awoke with a fart, snorted and sat up. Then he took a can of soda from his luggage and drank it in under a minute. He belched and more of his mouth-stink wafted my way. Then he began pacing the small territory of our train car. Like a fat, hairy pinball bouncing back and forth alongside the length of my supine body. When he moved toward my face, I caught his eyes. He seemed awake, but was he? Maybe he was a sleepwalker who chugged soda unconsciously. Maybe there was no consciousness behind those eyes. Maybe he was looking at me through the prism of dreams. That might explain the mildly psychotic look on his grotesque face, but it didn't matter—I wasn't getting any rest, maybe ever again.

In that sad excuse for a bed with that repulsive man astir, I knew I was getting ill. I could feel the sickness creeping into my cells. His breath, his body odor, his farts, his entire disgusting being—it was weakening me. *No, no, no... don't get sick! Lisbon! Wine! Cigarettes! Pastries! Fado! It's all waiting for you in a few hours. Just hang in there!*

He paced some more and stopped, again a few inches from my face. Did he wake up? I didn't know. There no way to communicate with him. We didn't speak the same language and, anyway, I was no longer sure the thing before me was human. He looked like some bulbous creature in sweat pants and suspenders that had been summoned from Hell, a rejected Cenobite not cool enough to hang with Pinhead—Butterball's lesser cousin. I wasn't sure what he was doing, but stationary fat fuck scared me more than pacing fat fuck. My left hand slid toward the only thing close to a weapon I had with me, *Infante's Inferno*. A 410-page hardback, it was hefty enough to do some damage. The fat fuck stood there for an interminable span of time. I held onto to *Infante's Inferno*, ready to swing the tome at the bastard's head. Thankfully, he went back to his bunk. I stayed still and ready, book in hand until the now familiar atrocious snores returned, along with the reek of his steady breath.

Lisbon was a sunny, welcoming sight. The apartment we'd rented was on a hill near a castle with some lovely views. Chris and D.C. were eager to hit the main part of the city, but I was ill. They didn't believe me. They'd managed to get some sleep, albeit not much, and they decided that the rotten train ride called for immediate fun.

"Go without me," I said. I needed rest. Cassandra went in search of medicine. In a few hours, I was better, and we met the others at an outdoor café where we drank red wine and watched the locals sing Fado. I sat with my future wife, old pals, some wine, beautiful music, and genuine joy. It remains one of my happiest nights and the last time I felt that level of affection for one of those men I once considered a friend.

On Avoiding Street Boxing

1999, Chicago, IL

I was sitting in a café reading Umberto Eco's great novel, *The Name of the Rose*. An acquaintance, Pierre, walked in with an attractive girl in tow. He said a version of my name rather boisterously: "VINNY!"

I cringed.

"Meet my fiancé!" he said. "She's from your homeland."

He meant Italy, but I wasn't in the mood to acknowledge that he'd travelled to Europe—that he'd, in fact, spent the entire summer there—or that he met a gorgeous Italian girl whom he'd managed to trick into a relationship.

"You mean Chicago?" I said.

Pierre looked hurt. We closed the conversation quickly and they walked to a table of their own. I opened *The Name of the Rose* and then immediately closed it, suddenly in no mood for anything Italian.

As with so many other books, I'll associate Pierre with *The Name of the Rose*, though when I think of him, I can't help but recall the last time I saw him, on Southport and Altgeld near my old apartment, the one Fern moved into without asking. She was with me. We were walking home after dinner when a few young men approached.

"Hey bitch, wanna box?" asked a kid who reeked of marijuana. He was muscular and, from the look on his face, I was convinced he wasn't just having fun with me. A few other rough looking youths surrounded him. One of them apologized.

"Sorry, he's all fucked up. Don't box with him."

"I wasn't planning on it," I said.

"C'mon, bitch," said the pot reeking thug.

"Chill," his friend said.

"Naw, fuck that!"

I anticipated a punch, but before the kid could throw one, Pierre emerged from behind the gaggle of toughs.

"Vinny!" he said, joining my side. I welcomed his presence, as it seemed to confuse the thug. To further push away the likelihood of getting my ass kicked, I started talking to Pierre as if we were closer than we were. I never really liked the guy, but damn if I wasn't going to grab hold of this life raft.

"How are you? Did you marry that beautiful Italian woman I last saw you with? Lucky devil."

"What's up?" asked my would-be sparring partner. "You ready to box?"

"Pierre, please meet some of the neighborhood kids," I said. Pierre looked confused. Then he extended his hand and introduced himself. The thugs didn't know what to do. The one who'd tried to calm his friend down took Pierre's hand. His friends laughed.

"Well, you all seem to be hitting it off, so I'll leave you. Nice seeing you, Pierre. Say hello to the missus."

Fern, who'd been silent through the whole affair, walked alongside me toward the apartment. I never looked back to see how Pierre got along with his new friends. Part of me fears that he got mercilessly beaten, and I do indeed feel bad about ditching him, but he was always the sort of happy-go-lucky jerk that fell into opportunities and skated effortlessly through life. He probably talked his way out of a fight. A rationalization, sure, but how would we get through our days without rationalizing bad behavior?

I never saw Pierre again. Maybe the luck on which he coasted his entire young life came to an end on that bit of Southport a few years before the area was completely rid of the last trace of its rough, working class past.

Sorry, Pierre, wherever you are.

The Mad Russian's Letter

2009, Chicago, IL

Matvey arrived in the United States of America somewhere in his teens. Maybe his twenties. I don't know the exact date. There's a lot I don't know about him. He was secretive; when it came to personal details, even his closest friends were on a need-to-know basis.

That stated, I took it as a compliment that he let me see his apartment, a studio in Rogers Park that contained the sum of his possessions: some clothes, a transistor radio, two 60 pound dumbbells, a futon, and the only five books he considered worth owning: *The Collected Works of Edgar Allen Poe*, Twain's *A Connecticut Yankee in King Arthur's Court*, A condensed edition of Gibbon's *Rise and Fall of the Roman Empire*, E.M. Cioran's *The Trouble with Being Born*, and John Kennedy Toole's *A Confederacy of Dunces*.

He had no bank account.

"Bankers are crooks!"

As we were preparing to exit his apartment and relocate to a nearby café, he asked me to look the other way. I assumed this was so he could fish some money from a secret spot.

"Banks are for blood and semen. Not money."

Though he didn't trust me enough to share all the details of his life, I knew a few things. He was born in Moscow. His father, Sergei, was an artist of some renown who had sketched portraits of the Silver Age Russian writers. His pictures of Mayakovsky and Akhmatova had been reprinted in various Soviet publications. Sergei's biggest claim to fame was a painting inspired by Bulgakov's

The Master and Margarita that was used for the cover of an early edition of the great novel. The painting contained images of Christ and Pilate, which the publisher decided was fittingly scandalous in the atheist country. Inspired by this success, Sergei painted another picture featuring a gun totting black cat and a naked redhead. This netted different reactions and was, according to Matvey, the beginning of his family's troubles.

"They kicked us out of the country. They took everything. They still owe my father for work they stole. I'm filing a suit against the government, Putin, and anyone else I can link to this travesty. Thieves! They're all thieves!"

Matvey asked me to review his written complaint against the Russian government. I'm not sure why. He was a lawyer and quite familiar with proper legal syntax. Nevertheless, he valued my opinion. That or he wanted to share something with me, something he felt should be widely known. His father was a political refugee, an artist robbed of his recognition. His name deserved to be on many lips. I didn't need to know what year Matvey was born or when exactly he came to America or how his mother had died, but his father's talent was something I absolutely had to understand.

It took some time, but I got more out of him. I learned that his family travelled from the Soviet Union to Switzerland and then to Italy before settling in the States. Matvey spoke fluent Italian, a fact he shared with me when he learned that my family came from an area he'd visited. I mentioned Matvey's Italian fluency to a barista at Starbucks who made our daily coffee and with whom Matvey had developed a slight familiarity. I assumed he'd have no problem with the barista knowing this small fact. I was wrong.

"Oh wow, say something in Italian!" the moon-faced barista demanded.

He refused her request and departed without paying. I covered the bill and left a handsome tip, scrambling to catch up to my friend. Later, when we were alone, he reprimanded me for telling the barista about his multilingualism.

"No one needs to know these things," he said. "No one!"

"I'm sorry."

"Bah!" he said and waved his hands in my face.

Matvey was technically my boss. One of them, at least. I worked as a legal assistant for a small law firm where he was an associate attorney. He remains one of the few lawyers I've met who didn't speak condescendingly to the support staff or consider themselves above anyone else simply because they passed the bar exam. First year associates fresh from law school often adopt the persona of asshole attorney, but Matvey, for all his standoffishness, refused to put himself above others. This humility may have been the product of an uncertain upbringing, or it may have simply come from his tremendous, albeit guarded, heart. Either way, it was endearing.

The other attorneys thought him something of an oddity—he never joined them for steak dinners or trips to the bar after work. They shunned him, assigning him research tasks that kept him hidden in his small office. Matvey was never allowed to conduct depositions or make courtroom appearances. He was too unpredictable and wouldn't suffer fools gladly. There was no telling what he might say to a condescending judge or what harsh comment might find itself permanently recorded by a court stenographer.

I don't flatter myself that I'm somehow more interesting than any of the attorneys in that office. Matvey, desperate for company despite his reservations, sought me out so that he might maintain some semblance of human interaction. I was safe; I didn't ask a lot of questions.

The attorneys wondered about my unusual friend.

"What's with that guy?"

"What do you two talk about anyway?" I was asked as if an attorney would have no common ground with a mere support staffer. Realizing that saying anything to them about Matvey would nullify our friendship, I ignored their questions.

I feel the need to explain our relationship. We were friends in the sense that no one could ever really be Matvey's friend. He was kind despite his disdain for most people, but anyone he chose to associate with needed to have a high threshold for eccentric behavior. Matvey, ever the suspicious animal, let me get close but in no way was he ever vulnerable. We were only as close as he'd let us be.

We had lunch together a few times a week. He almost always paid. Every morning we went for coffee and a cookie. During this time, Matvey would regale me with truncated episodes of his life. Whenever he felt that things were becoming more familiar than his sense of reserve could handle, he'd end the tale by saying, "but that is not of any concern." His tone was authoritative and bureaucratic, much the way I imagined the cold officials of his native country sounded. From these snippets, I filled in the details of his biography, the flight from the Soviet Union and then the departure from Europe to the United States, specifically to New Orleans—Matvey's favorite city—and his education at Tulane. Perhaps his time in New Orleans contributed to his love of *A Confederacy of Dunces*. He once told me that Ignatius Reilly was the greatest character ever conceived. When I asked him about Raskolnikov, he laughed.

"Dostoevsky's books are miserable. They are the garbage I was forced to endure as a child. Sermonizing trash. Drivel masquerading as profound."

I, a lover of Russian literature, pressed him, but he had no use for my literary heroes. Mark Twain, according to him, was infinitely wiser than any Russian writer. I tried to springboard off this comment and point out how Twain, Bulgakov, and Tolstoy all made the devil a character in their last books. This did not impress Matvey.

"Tolstoy: aristocratic phony. Bulgakov? Farce and folly."

Even though Bulgakov had inspired his father's art, Matvey wasn't interested. He saw Russian novels as bloated and preachy, unworthy of discussion, especially with an American. This was true of anything Russian. I expressed interest in someday going to Moscow. Matvey's response: "Watch your wallet if you do."

While he had a certain contempt for Russia, Matvey could be proud of his countrymen. He informed me that a Russian had co-created Google, beaming as he read aloud from an interview with Sergey Brin. He also expressed pride that the Russians were the first to go into space and never shied away from praising Russian food over all American fare (save for gumbo, which, he gladly pointed out, was more European than American).

I suspect that Matvey made less money than the other attorneys. This may have been because he was given limited responsibilities, but could've been due to "just cause," as the partners called it, pronounced closer to "just cuz" as in "just cuz I don't like him."

Matvey refused to "kiss another person's posterior" to get ahead. "Hard work should be all that matters. If I cannot get anywhere by honest work than I will go nowhere."

He toiled at every project, generating good results. He was serious about his job, often refusing to speak with me during the time allocated to research. Despite his dedication and focus, his efforts were never really rewarded. Yes, he received a paycheck like the rest of us, but the other associates got larger bonuses than Matvey, assuming he got one at all. Research was simply not as showy as court appearances. The partners may have understood Matvey's contributions, but they regarded him as an oddball. A hard worker, but not to be let into the club.

I expected Matvey to be more upset about his isolation from his colleagues, but he shook off my concerns. We were in a deli in the Loop eating sub sandwiches ("indigestible slop") and chatting about the office. Though he was reluctant to get into a personal discussion, he relished office gossip.

"Boobla Khan is up to something," he said.

"Who?"

"Boobla. You know him." He gave me a look that dictated I infer without asking a follow up question.

"Can you give me a hint?" I asked.

"You study poetry?"

"Yes."

"What are the first lines of Coleridge's 'Kubla Khan'?"

"'In Xanadu did Kubla Khan...'"

"Yes?"

"'A stately pleasure-dome decree.'"

"Exactly! Who in this office has created a pleasure-dome?"

"Oh..."

The senior partner of the firm had recently bought a liquor cabinet and was fond of smoking marijuana in his office, an act he assumed went undiscovered despite the skunky odor that filled the workplace. There were also reports of sexual harassment from three separate female employees. Rumor had it that sex workers visited him at the office whenever he had to work late.

"Another man's pleasure-dome. That is where we spend our workdays."

"Okay, so why is he *Boobla* Khan?"

"You don't understand this pun? He's a boob! Plain and simple!"

Matvey went on to make other bizarre comments about our boss and coworkers, the culmination being his complaint about the lack of sense they displayed and their irritating manner of yelling at each other from across a room. ("Why are you all so loud?") It was then that I tried to make a comment about his lack of recognition, convinced that doing so would solidify my position as friend. He waved it away with his large hands.

"I don't see ambition as a virtue," he said.

"But it must bother you when—"

"It doesn't!"

When he raised his voice, I knew the conversation was over. We finished our sandwiches in quiet. It was only after I offered to buy him a coffee that he spoke.

"The problem with Americans is that you all think money cures everything."

Despite this sentiment, he accepted my offer. The recently rebuffed barista fulfilled our request for two double espressos and a cookie while we thumbed through the remains of newspapers abandoned on the counter. Matvey began chuckling.

"Look at this," he said. "The mayor wants to bring the Olympics to Chicago."

"I know."

"The ultimate demonstration of stupidity."

"I'm not in favor of the games coming here either. It'll mean razing buildings and displacing residents and—"

"No, no, no," he said. "Not the Olympics coming to Chicago, that is not the stupidity. It's the Olympics itself! If the games come to Chicago that will only mean that the ultimate spectacle of man's stupidity will be on display in our very own city! Think of it: athletes will descend upon us, as will spectators. There will be celebrations and banners and all kinds of ridiculous behavior. People will cheer when their country wins a medal. Nationalism will swamp us! It will be like Rome burning. When the time comes, I don't wish to be here for Nero's fiddling."

Chicago lost the bid for the Olympics. Matvey may have delighted in Mayor Daley's failure, but we were out of contact by then. I'd left the law firm after a long time of trying to become something other than an office drone. Matvey stayed behind in the pleasure-dome, sifting through statutes and precedents in search of a kernel of information that might benefit one of the other lawyers. No longer in proximity, and neither of us being fond of telephones, we ceased contact.

I learned of Matvey's death during an impromptu lunch with one of the clerks from the law firm. We ran into each other in Andersonville, a trendy part of the north side, and, perhaps because neither of us could come up with an excuse, decided to grab a coffee. The conversation quickly exhausted the expected questions: How are things? Who's been fired? Did the boss win his sexual harassment suit?

During the course of dishing on former colleagues, I learned the details of Matvey's demise. He left the firm about six months after my departure. There were rumblings about office relocation. The boss wanted to save money on rent and be closer to his home and began looking for space in the northern suburbs. Matvey decided not to follow.

"Everyone tried to tell him that this was just an idea, that no relocation plans had really been made, but he didn't care. He quit."

"Where'd he go?" I asked.

"Nowhere. He couldn't find a new job. Not in this economy. No one's hiring lawyers right now. Especially not lawyers like *him*."

Matvey decided to go solo. He worked freelance for other firms picking up work where he could, but he no longer had health insurance. When he contracted pneumonia the following winter, he had nowhere else to go but the county hospital, the last place anyone wants to be. It wasn't long before he died surrounded by overworked strangers.

"Jesus, I had no idea."

"His father was supposed to have a memorial for him, but I don't know if he ever did."

"Shit. Maybe it hasn't happened yet," I said.

"I dunno… It's been a while."

Later that day, I checked the Internet and found a brief obituary, but there was no mention of a service. I thought about trying to locate Matvey's father. I gave up on the idea when I remembered that he only spoke Russian and "enough English to complain." If a memorial was ever held, I'd missed it.

That was a few years ago. Today when I opened my copy of *The Idiot*, a book I'd attempted to read while at the firm, I found a short letter sandwiched between pages 347 and 348.

Vincenzo,

Why do you persist in reading this rubbish? Do you think there is some secret in these pages, that this psychological rambling and phony philosophizing will reveal some truth that will shatter your primitive understanding of the universe? I am sorry to tell you that you are wasting your time. There is no truth to be found here. Just the ravings of a syphilitic gambling addict. Ignatius Reilly is a greater character than any you will find in this bloated nonsense. But your insistence is not your fault. You were raised to believe in the exotic and see nonsense such as this as inherently valuable simply because it comes from a different culture. In this case, the culture is sick and, in studying the work of a sick culture, your own is infected. This is what you went to a university to read, the manifestation of an advanced disease.

Well, if you must, enjoy your sickness.

M.

I put the letter back inside the book, closed it, cried.

Poetry Will Save Us

During my lunch break, I ran into a friend, a woman who was my professor when I was an undergrad at the school where I now work. She was my favorite teacher—smart, funny, didn't take shit—and assigned great stuff. Thanks to her syllabi I read Salman Rushdie, Ciaran Carson, Medbh McGuckian, Seamus Heaney, Paul Muldoon, Ngũgĩ wa Thiong'o, Nuruddin Farah, and Edna O'Brien, many of these names I wouldn't have encountered on my own.

While chatting near the department mailboxes, she told me that she's assigned far less reading in her classes since the days when I was a student, and considerably less poetry.

"No one wants to read it," she said.

"But they're English majors."

"They are, but the evaluations always say 'More videos.'"

"But why'd they sign up to earn an English degree if they want to watch videos?"

"That's the trend in education—more visual learning. I read somewhere that the average person only has about an eight second attention span. It was probably only twelve seconds when you were a student."

She was joking, but there's a good chance that she's correct; the average individual probably can't pay attention to anything for longer than a few seconds before they get fidgety and pull out their smartphone. Expecting students to read a novel a week is apparently asking too much. Oh, the joys of the 21st century, the age of immediacy and distraction!

Vincent Francone

I know this applies to me as well. It's appalling how much time I waste online, how short my attention span has become. I used to spend my leisure hours with my face in a book. It was a lovely way of passing the time after a day of work or even when waiting in line at the grocery store. I would take on ambitious, hefty tomes without once thinking about the TV I was missing or the emails to be addressed. These were the halcyon days when the internet was a thing I had to go to a library or a cybercafé to access, back before people expected instant replies to their text messages. It was also the time when television was utter crap. It didn't seem like there was anything worth watching, so I read a lot. Now I can't believe how good TV has become. Those people proclaiming this to be the golden age of TV are, it turns out, quite right. Who wants to read the poetry of Osip Mandelstam when I can binge watch *The Wire*?

In my ENG 101 class, I sometimes ask my students to read a series of essays about the effects of technology on culture. We start with Neil Postman and then read a little bit of Nicholas Carr before getting to the biting comments of Andrew Keen. One point that usually comes up after I assign Carr is that his essay is too long.

"It took forever," a student once said.

"I stopped reading after the fifth page," another confessed.

"What do you think Carr's purpose is? Why did he write an essay this long?"

They usually answer that Carr is an old guy who thinks everything he has to say is important. This from a generation that thinks every mundane thing they get up to is worth sharing on Instagram.

"Okay," I say, "so what's he trying to argue? What's his thesis?"

"That the internet is ruining our ability to concentrate on anything longer than a text message," someone will venture.

"So, if you had a hard time reading this essay, a whopping nine pages, then Carr has proven his thesis."

This doesn't seem as mind-blowing to them as it does to me.

Despite coming off a bit preachy, I confess to my students that I can relate. Lately I get frustrated if a book is longer than 200 pages. I read in short bursts, alternating between printed book and laptop screen. I squeeze YouTube videos and Facebook posts between the chapters of whatever I'm supposed to be reading. I wonder what kind of student I'd be if I were back on the other side of the classroom. And I worry about my ability to focus, especially as I'm now middle-aged. I can't imagine my attention span getting any better, especially if I continue to drink large portions of whiskey and spend considerable amounts of time online.

As is often the case, the solution is poetry.

The poet Nick Laird made a nice point: in the age of Twitter, poetry is the best antidote we have to the trend of immediacy over contemplation. It requires patience, can't really be skimmed, and it's almost always necessary to reread a poem.

I've been reading a lot of poetry to reverse the damage technology has done to my attention span. I reread some Seamus Heaney and then Nick Laird's first book, then went back to Whitman and Dickinson and Robert Lowell and John Berryman. Then Cesar Vallejo and Vicente Huidobro to get a reminder of the strange possibilities of literature. Then I did some research into poets I've not read before. One of them is Rosemary Tonks, whose posthumous collection of poems, *Bedouin of the London Evening*, led me to the Seminary Co-op bookstore, pride of the University of Chicago's intellectual community. There I found the book, which I've wanted to read ever since I saw a review where the young Tonks was quoted as saying, "The main duty of the poet is to excite – to send the senses reeling." I quite agree.

Sadly, I disliked the book. The poems have some flashes of brilliance suggesting that a more mature writer would've made use of her natural talent and produced something stronger, but Tonks' work is a bit callow and ultimately dispensable, making it hard to disagree with Rosemary the older fundamentalist Christian who denounced her youthful writing and suppressed her poems. The experience left me bummed.

But I don't regret the money I spent on the book ($26.00 plus tax). I'll likely not reread the book anytime soon, but the hours I spent laboring over the surreal poems were not wasted. I take a lot of chances on poetry, and most of the time they don't pay off. Poems should, indeed, blow the top of your head off, but often they're dull, affected, over-wrought or, worse, dashed off and trite. Yet I still search through them looking for the one poem—hell, the one line—that will remind me that the effort is worthwhile.

Writers often speak of the struggle to produce one goddamn line that is close to good. Hours spent in front of the computer, booze within reach and eyes near tears, all in vain when nothing much comes. But when it clicks—oh, what magic! What a thrill. There's nothing like it. I know full well what writers mean when they rhapsodize about their specific form of self-abuse. But the same can be said of reading poems, which requires a level of focus rare in this modern, tech-saturated culture of ours. I'm often left feeling empty and unengaged by the poems I read, but when I do stumble on that rare wonderful creation, the search is more than validated.

I liken this process to what Dostoevsky seemed to be up to in many of his works: the struggle to understand what it means to be a soul in search of God. Reading poetry is a spiritual quest, a meditation on the unnamable entity that fortifies us against the collection of absolute shit accumulating just outside the door. How to sustain sanity against it all? Some look to God. Others look to poetry.

This is not to say that I find comfort and meaning in Yeats on par with what the average zealot gets from the New Testament. But I do see something beautiful and mysterious in Yeats' best work that suggests a force greater than my understanding. I'm probably not anywhere close to explaining it here, but I'm often invigorated by a poem to the extent that I can face whatever hell is waiting for me the moment I set foot out of the apartment.

Someone once called poetry "language elevated," meaning (I guess) that the language of poetry is higher than that of prose, certainly of everyday speech. I don't 100% agree with this blanket statement, but I do recall the words of Joseph Brodsky: "By failing to read or listen to poets, society dooms itself to inferior modes of articulation, those of the politician, the salesman, or the charlatan." No wonder Trump has soared so high.

Hester Prynne Makes a Great Ashtray

1992, Worth, IL

"I don't feel like working today."

"Me neither," I said.

The first voice belongs to Red, real name Mike. I have no idea what his last name is. I knew it once, but it's been forgotten in the years since we worked side-by-side. I wish I knew his full name. I might try to find him on Facebook, but what would be the point? He's likely married with a crop of children and a mortgage and a lousy job and health concerns and dreams of escaping the life he's made.

Red lived in the Mt. Greenwood neighborhood of Chicago, a working-class community, very close-knit and friendly so long as you're not wearing a Cubs jersey or African-American. I had friends from the area, most of them probably all cops or firemen or bartenders now. Red worked part time as a barback when not manning a barcoding machine with me during the day in a warehouse that made junk mail. The bar he worked at wouldn't admit anyone under the age of 23. I was 21, but Red promised he'd get me in. That promise went unfulfilled; the night I tried to get in, the bartender told me to get fucked.

"But I know Red," I said.

"Who the hell is Red?"

The next day, while I fed letters into the machine and he caught them on the other side, Red told me I should've asked for Mike.

"No one calls me Red outside of this place."

We called him Red because there are too many Mikes in the world. No one was just Mike. There was Mike D., Mike K., Mike "Chuck" Connors, "Marty" Mike Dell, and a series of Micks and Mickeys. And there was Red, the funniest guy I've ever met.

Barcoding is dull. The above description is about all there is to it: one machine, two workers, no skill aside from rudimentary hand-eye coordination. For eight hours a day, Red and I manned the barcoding machine. To combat the boredom, we told jokes, though mostly Red told them and I laughed. I couldn't keep up with him. And his jokes were objectively bad, though, in the middle of the worst kind of blue-collar drudgery, every one of them cracked me up.

"Did you hear about the farmer who was out standing in his field?"

I mean, it's so old it's got whiskers on it, but when Red dropped that glorious pun on me, I nearly doubled over with laughter.

"Hey Vince, know what 6.9 is? No? 69 interrupted by a period."

"Dude... gross."

"Okay, okay... how bout this one—How many psychiatrists does it take to change a light bulb?"

"No idea."

"One, but the light bulb has to want to change."

Laughter.

"You know how many Vietnam vets it takes to change a light bulb?"

"No, how many?"

"FUCK YOU! YOU WEREN'T THERE, MAN!"

Unrestrained laughter.

"Okay, last one—How many boring people does it take to change a light bulb?"

"How many?"

In a monotone voice Red said, "Just one."

That may be the lamest joke ever told. I snorted with laughter.

Red decided to act on our mutual disinclination toward work. After declaring that he wasn't in the mood to man the barcoder, he lifted the lid of the machine and started pulling wires.

"What the fuck?" I asked.

"Relax," he said. "I went to DeVry. I know what I'm doing."

Red then started monkeying with the belt and some of the more fragile parts until the machine was, as he put it, "Sincerely screwed."

"Now run some mail through," he said.

I did as instructed until the barcoder made a terrible whining sound. We killed the power and watched the big contraption shake and die. Bill, a slovenly forklift driver, caught that part of the show and told us he'd get our supervisor. We thanked him.

Our super was a nice enough guy, but in over his head. He'd been given three departments to oversee. Of them, ours was the least interesting. Barcoding was where people started or ended up after they'd proven they couldn't work elsewhere. The super wasn't about to devote an extra minute to us, which worked to our advantage. Essentially, so long as we got a reasonable amount of mail coded, we were left alone. That meant we could work hard for the first half of the day and do next to nothing during the second. Or one of us could take a long lunch and the other would cover for him.

Red liked to take long lunches and often ended up down the street at the tavern. When he was gone so long that even our lackluster supervisor took notice, I'd send one of the bundlers, a comely Polish girl who knew only a handful of English words, to get him. Red was in love with her, or so he told me. He always followed her back to work.

"I love that girl," he'd say upon his return.

"So ask her out."

"I did. Twice."

"And?"

"She can't understand me. She just smiles and looks away."

After waiting around for several minutes, the super arrived to inspect the state of the machine.

"Jesus, what happened?"

"Don't know, boss," Red said. "We sent some mail through and it started smoking."

"God, that smoke stinks."

"I know—like garlic, gas, and unwashed ass," said Red.

Our super shook his head and told us to wait in the break room while he got someone to fix it. And that's where we stayed for the next six hours. No one came for us and we weren't about to go looking for our super. We figured we were following orders. No need reminding anyone that we were supposed to be working. Instead we sat in the break room and let our streams of constant cigarette smoke add several coats of yellow to the originally white walls. I drank three cups of the worst coffee on Earth before Red remembered that he had a flask on him. I wasn't much of a whiskey drinker then, but I wasn't opposed to Red improving the lousy coffee by "making it a wee more Irish."

"Fucking Irish. You guys…"

"Yeah, and you know what they say about the Irish? Where there's one there's a hundred. We're like rabbits. And we multiply everything." To prove his point, he swallowed his cup's worth of whiskey and poured more for both of us. "See. Multiplying before your eyes."

"Like the loaves and fishes. A miracle, Father Red."

"Keep drinking and soon you'll be seeing two of me."

We carried on loafing, drinking, joking. It was somewhere in hour five when Red asked me about the book I was carrying.

"Hawthorne," I told him. "*Scarlet Letter*. You read it?"

"No, but I know about it. Cheating wife gets knocked up, right?"

"Yeah, and has to wear the big red A."

"Harsh."

I agreed. He asked if it was any good. I told him I was enjoying it.

"I think my sister read it," he said. "She had to for school. Hated it."

"No one in my class likes it. They all bitch about it, even to the teacher's face."

"Aren't they into that stuff?"

"We're all supposed to be English majors, yeah. But even English majors hate *The Scarlet Letter*."

"I don't get it. Why'd they sign up for that degree if they hate the material?"

"They just don't want to read anything that seems like work."

"Lazy."

"Right? It's a shame what the world's coming to. Lazy, unmotivated pricks."

Eventually, Red nodded off. The coffee did a good job fighting the booze, but a light nap sounded nice. I figured I'd rest my eyes while my ears stayed alert for the sound of anyone crashing our party. Best laid plans, as they say, for I did, of course, fall deeply asleep. The sound of our super charging into the break room woke us.

"What's going on here?"

"Sorry, boss," Red said. "Just checking the eyelids for holes."

"Whatever. You guys can go home early. The machine's fucked. No way it'll be fixed until tomorrow. Clock out. You can make up the time over the weekend if you want."

We didn't want to make up the time, a mere two hours. We figured the lost money was worth the joy of having been paid for six hours of goofing off. There would never be a day like that again. Machines can only be sabotaged so many times before the boss gets wise. This was a day stolen. Our day. The best day of work I could imagine.

"What now?" I asked.

Red stretched until his back cracked. "Lunch?"

"Sure."

I stood up and grabbed *The Scarlet Letter*. A neglected cigarette had left ash and burn marks on the cover.

"Shit!" I showed Red the book. "We could've burned the place to the ground."

"Naw. The book wouldn't have caught fire."

"How do you know?"

"Well, it didn't, did it? If it was going to catch fire, it would've."

"When did you put your cigarette on my book, anyway?"

"I dunno. Might've put one down for a second then passed out. Sorry. But I'll say this: Hester Prynne makes a great ashtray."

"How do you know her name?" I asked.

"Huh?"

"I thought you never read it."

"Well, I told you I knew about it. It's not like you have to read everything to know a thing or two."

Red was fired a few weeks later. The super never said anything about the broken barcoder, which anyone with the slightest understanding of the machine would see was intentionally busted. Rather, Red got canned after he failed to return from lunch. Even the beautiful Polish girl couldn't get him back from the bar.

"I was about twenty-three sheets to the wind," he told me the next day, right before he was asked to clock out and never return. We hugged. I'd never hugged a man who wasn't my father. It should've been weird. This was the southwest side. Any action remotely affectionate between men would be met with screams of "Faggot!" But we hugged in front of the whole floor with the forklift drivers, the bundlers, the supers, all of them watching.

"I'll swing by next week. We'll grab a bite. Whaddya say?"

I told Red that sounded great, but I never saw the guy again.

On Not Reading Books

Tsundoku. That's what the Japanese call this practice of buying and hoarding books that never get read. I'm no speaker of Japanese, and my attempt at pronunciation is surely flawed, but I'll admit that the Japanese word is beautiful in a way my phrase is not. *Soft lunacy*... an inelegant description, but it works for me. Not quite the gentle madness, though a malady nonetheless.

If we're telling the truth, aren't we all a little guilty of tsundoku/soft lunacy? Don't many of us have books on our shelves that we, in theory, want to read but, in practice, don't ever touch? I've kept a lot of philosophy, science, and even religious studies texts that I don't plan to read any time soon (translation: ever). But I like the books. I don't keep them to impress visitors with my alleged intellectual rigor, as no one really comes over to visit. No, I keep them because their mere presence makes me happy. That I could pick one up and look up a concept or read a few pages and learn something about the stoics or the Buddhists or string theory is affirming.

There's a bigger concept to be unpacked: the idea of a book is sometimes better than the book itself. Coleridge wrote in his introduction to "Kubla Khan" of the person from Porlock who interrupted his writing and, thus, ruined what could've been an epic poem. Scholars have debated the truth of this tale—it sounds like a cop out. *Oh, I was going to write a long, brilliant poem but this pesky visitor distracted me and I lost the vision.* Yeah, sure. Coleridge, you were just being lazy. Or not. Maybe Coleridge, in suggesting a longer version of

"Kubla Khan" that was lost in the ether of his faulty memory, was creating the ultimate poem, one more grand and beautiful than any written before or since. As readers of the shorter, fragmentary "Kubla Khan", we're forced to imagine what else could've been written had that jerk from Porlock not come a-knockin'.

The fuzzy idea of a brilliant poem is better than any written poem could be, as poetry, by its nature, is always a failed attempt to render a vision or idea or experience into words. A lot of great poems succeed by suggesting something and drawing the reader in through the recognition of an intangible. In that sense, "Kubla Khan"—the part that never got written—is the best poem ever. We can imagine a bombastic or sublime work that inspires and delights, a poem that astonishes us, that drives us wild. A poem worthy of the overtaxed word "awesome." Sounds wonderful. Why ruin it by writing it down?

Similarly, some of the books in my library are best experienced by imagining their contents. Even books written by people whose other works I admire… I neglect them as well. Case in point: *The Irish for No* by Ciaran Carson.

Let's back up and discuss Carson's *Belfast Confetti*. As an undergraduate, I read this collection of poems while taking a class called *Imagining Terror*. I was very excited to take this class. I knew we'd be reading Salman Rushdie and Seamus Heaney and Joseph Conrad, not to mention some books by African and South Asian writers, literature an undergrad is rarely exposed to. Carson's book ended up being not only my favorite of the semester but the subject of my final paper and, after a second joyous read, a solid entry on my Ten Best Ever list. It's the book I go back to when I want to remember why I love poetry.

Being a soft lunatic, I went looking for other books by Carson. Most were easy to find—I snatched up *First Language* via Amazon.com and found *Shamrock Tea* at a used shop—though it took flying to Washington, D.C. to get a few others.

April 2007, Washington, D.C.

Carson, along with Michael Longley and Paul Muldoon, was giving a talk at Georgetown University on the literature of Northern Ireland. No one would go with me to the event, so I flew by myself to the nation's capital to geek out for a day. Of course, I bought a pile of books and had the authors sign them. Carson was not interested in signing books or talking to his fans (well, at least not to me), but he was a good sport about it inasmuch as he didn't refuse any requests for an autograph, just sat and looked somewhat put-upon during the book signing process.

I admired Carson even more after this event. He was a *serious* writer, a brilliant poet and novelist—he wasn't interested in being a star. I left D.C. with a renewed drive to collect everything he'd written.

The thing is, his second book, the one that's supposed to be his groundbreaking work, *The Irish for No*, is difficult to find. At least it was in 2007. Today, an Amazon.com search has revealed available used copies for upwards of $40. But in 2007, when I was obsessing over Carson's work, I couldn't find a copy of what critics were calling his best, most important collection. I managed to get it by purchasing his *Collected Poems* about a year later. Finally, I could dive into *The Irish for No*!

But I didn't. I looked at the table of contents and saw that the book, indeed, was represented in this collection. But I stuck the *Collected Poems* on a shelf and haven't taken it down since.

What's stopping me from reading *The Irish for No*? The very idea that it's not as fantastic as I've built it up to be. As long as I don't read the book, it will remain unquestionably brilliant. And I admire Carson too much to have this book, this thing I've unfairly elevated, be anything short of perfect. This book is my Schrödinger's cat—if I open that box, I may find that the cat is dead. Can't have that on my conscience.

Jim Harrison's Brand of Masculinity

1995, Chicago, IL

Paige was a quiet girl from Michigan who loved Jim Harrison's books, especially *Dalva*.

"Every day I wonder, what would Dalva do in this situation?" she said as we were browsing in a bookshop. "You should read this one for starters." She handed me a copy of *Farmer*.

Being a young urban idiot, I had no intention of reading a book about a farmer, but I agreed to buy it and promised I'd give it a shot. When the clerk asked if I needed a bag, Paige butted in.

"He doesn't," she said, ever the good environmentalist.

We walked north on Broadway, me carrying *Farmer* and trying to figure out how I'd get a kiss. She had a boyfriend, though considering the man was in his sixties, "boyfriend" seemed an improper term. I learned about her oldmanfriend after we'd kissed the first time. She was staying in the shithole apartment I shared with some friends until she could find a place of her own. After stumbling in from a party, she found me asleep on the couch. A few nudges later, I was up and angry.

"What the hell is wrong with you?" I asked. She smiled and asked if I wanted to kiss her. Suddenly I was a lot less angry.

The kiss was pleasant but soon ruined by her confession that she had an oldmanfriend and shouldn't be doing this or anything further.

"Well, we already kissed once, so… a little more won't hurt, right?"

To my surprise, she agreed. We kissed until Carl, that bastard, woke up and interrupted us. He didn't realize what he'd done. Paige took his appearance as a sign that maybe she ought to say goodnight. The second she was gone, I turned to Carl and said, "I just kissed Paige. Go the fuck to bed."

"Dude... nice."

After he went back to his room, I knocked on Paige's door, but she wasn't interested. Our moment was gone.

I spent the next few weeks pursuing Paige, during which time I was told repeatedly to read *Farmer*. I delayed, spending time with Hemingway and Vonnegut instead. Eventually Paige moved out and I misplaced the book, though it turned up a few years later during a move. I have it now, still unread.

All these years later, I'm married to a woman who loves *Legends of the Fall*, cementing my suspicion that women are drawn to Jim Harrison's brand of masculinity, a sort of rugged bravado tempered by sensitivity. Harrison had no problem being vulnerable, even when he was drunk and coked up. One reviewer stated that no male writer writes women better than Harrison. My favorite of his author photos, aside from the recent ones where he looks like a zombie with a cigarette, is of him lying in a field with a little girl (presumably his daughter) on top of him, her folded arms on his shoulder, a tiny flower clutched in the teeth of her grin. Harrison is bulky with a walrus moustache, every bit the giant cuddly daddy a little girl could want.

Maybe that's it—maybe Paige was attracted to me because, like Harrison, I was a plump guy with big appetites. And it was usually after mutual indulgence of alcoholic appetites that I had any success with her.

After she moved out of my apartment, I went to her housewarming party, a bit of a bust. Few of her friends showed. Her roommate's companions seemed uninterested in her, or me for that matter. I'd brought some people with me, all of them doing their best to get drunk and eat the free food. Of them, Carl was most demonstrative and annoying, which only made Paige's roommate more irritated.

Paige finished her fourth beer and asked me if I wanted to go for a walk. Carl heard and assumed her invitation extended to all of us. He gathered his girlfriend, Anna, and accompanied Paige and me down Belden Avenue toward the lake. We got to the beach and all took a seat on the sand. It was very late, and the evening chill made Paige declare that she would tolerate the cold no longer. I expected her to leave, but instead she sat between my legs and pulled my coat over her. Carl was talking some dumb shit about a movie he'd just seen—I wasn't really listening to him or to Anna. All I could think was: *How the hell do I get rid of these two?*

After what felt like a very long time, the four of us left the beach. I was hoping the nighttime waves hitting the sand would provide a romantic setting, but I wasn't sure how to make any advances with Carl and Anna around. Paige helped me out; she stalled, walking slowly until Carl and Anna were far enough away. Then she kissed me.

It was nice, but I suddenly felt angry. We'd done this already. I tried to pursue her, but it went nowhere. And now, after a few beers, there I was conveniently ready to offer her validation.

I broke the kiss.

"What's wrong?"

"I dunno," I said. "Maybe this is a bad idea. You've got a, um, you know. Someone in your life."

"I told him."

"What?"

"I told him about you."

"What'd you say?"

"That I met someone. That I wanted to be with you. At least here in Chicago."

"And you'd be with him in…"

"Michigan."

"Right. I remember."

She paused, which made me angrier. "So, what'd he say?" I

asked.

"He's not happy about it. But he just said he doesn't want to know anything."

"That sounds…" I wasn't sure how it sounded. Tricky. Messy. Sure to end badly for all of us.

We walked back to her place. Nothing else happened. We just said goodnight and made some plans to get together the next afternoon. And we did, but it was an awkward lunch. Neither of us seemed to be able to tolerate the other. I wasn't so charming or handsome in the light of sober day. Her interrogation of the waitress irked me.

"Do you know if there's any lard in the muffins?"

"I'm…not sure," answered the waitress.

"Are the blueberry pancakes covered in compote or are the blueberries baked in?"

"Both, I think."

"Hmm… When was the tuna salad prepared?"

"In the kitchen."

"*When*, not *where!*"

Just order something and live with it, I thought.

We managed to talk about nothing of consequence and sipped coffee. The whole thing took forty minutes, enough time to say we'd actually met without prolonging anything. She left before me. I stayed at the café and read a book not written by Jim Harrison. One of the things we'd talked about was why I hadn't read *Farmer* yet. I told her I was getting around to it. That probably didn't help raise my stock.

That was the end of our brief not-quite-a-relationship, though Paige did call me a few months later. She was drunk. I asked her why she was calling.

"I wanted to say hi."

"No other reason?"

"What do you mean?"

"I mean," I said, "are you calling because you want to meet. You know—do you want what usually happens when you're drunk to happen?"

"Forget I called." *Click!*

So ended another romance. Wonder if that's how Jim Harrison would've handled it.

Revised Dialogue

July 2016, Chicago, IL

To combat the encroachment of middle-age deterioration, and in order to maintain my bad habits, I've started running. After a few weeks of sore muscles, running is getting easier, though not when I pass the little free libraries in the neighborhood. If I spy a book that I absolutely must have (for free!), then the run will either abruptly stop or I will attempt to jog back to my apartment with a tome in each hand.

One of the benefits of running is sweating out the toxins of the previous night's indulgence. I'm likely fooling myself if I think that a 20-minute jog around the neighborhood is doing much to combat a slice of pizza, two pints of ale, and a double whiskey, but running a bit allows me to maintain my illusion.

I heard that tears are also a form of releasing toxins. This may be bullshit, but the idea is that we feel better after a good cry because the body is expelling bad things via ocular secretion. I can't recall feeling better after any recent cry. Considering I've spent seven months crying and most of the last two months running, I should, in theory, be rid of all negative feelings. That I'm not rid of them must mean that my soul is as black as tar.

The little free library obsession has gotten out of hand. In addition to rerouting my run to accommodate the soft lunacy, last week I was driving down Albion past a book box under a viaduct next to a memorial for a college student who was shot last summer. This is not one of the better book boxes; most of the time it's filled with water damaged paperbacks and children's books. But, glancing past as I drove, I spied the unmistakable cover of the Vintage Books edition of *Ulysses*. I slammed on the breaks, upsetting the driver behind me. After waving an apology, I pulled over to snag James Joyce. Behind his opus was a copy of *Death in Venice and Other Stories* by Thomas Mann. My god! Two titans of 20th century European literature! For free!

There I was, just a few moments after a near car accident, greedily snatching a couple of books I already own and muttering "Mine, mine, mine."

The little free libraries are only the newest version of free books in my neighborhood. I live near Loyola University. When students move, they pitch the books they had to buy for last semester's classes. From the discarded material, I can surmise which books students dislike. They seem to dislike the Russians. I found a copy of *Crime and Punishment* the same day I moved into my apartment. I was walking past an alley just south of Pratt Blvd. and there was Dostoevsky just waiting for me. A few months later, while walking my dog, I found a copy of *The Idiot* in the same space.

As I walked toward the alley to claim *The Idiot*, a car sped up and nearly hit my little dog. This happens often, and most times I let it go and silently judge the drivers, but that day I was in no mood to tolerate this asshole's lack of concern.

The driver parked. I walked to his car and the following exchange took place (confession: I am writing this dialogue the way I wish it went, without the stammering and awkwardness and obscenity that plagued my actual admonishment of the careless driver, though I do believe this is accurate inasmuch as it captures the spirit of our conversation):

"Sir, you should take greater care not to speed through alleys, as you nearly struck me and my beloved dog."

"Excuse me, but who are you to criticize my driving? I do not recall any significant level of danger created by my actions."

"You may not realize it, but you were accelerating as you

approached the street, and, subsequently, I had to modify my gait so as to avoid your automobile."

"I think you exaggerate, citizen. My vehicle was not in any way threatening you or your canine."

"Sir, we disagree on that point."

"Indeed but consider this: you could be more polite—your manner of criticizing me is rude, abrupt, frankly un-neighborly."

"Well, how else might I have reacted?"

I began to walk away. The driver yelled: "Be sure to pick up your dog's feces!"

"What are you suggesting?"

"You feel entitled to criticize me. I should have the same right. It's called reciprocity."

"Ah, but here you are speculating on my possible inaction, whereas I witnessed your negligence. Clearly you see the two are not equal. Therefore, you are wrong to have made this exclamation."

"Well, I stand by my outrage—your actions were uncalled for."

"I feel otherwise. This conversation is now pointless. I will say good day to you, sir."

If only life was as elegantly phrased as fiction.

Kafkaesque Company and the Flying Henry Miller

1995, Chicago, IL

When she left, I had the apartment to myself, few distractions, no real demands on my time, and a lot of late nights alone.

I'd met Sophie in a poetry class when we were both in community college. She wasn't much for poems, but she took the class anyway as a means of broadening her knowledge.

"I thought it was important to know something about poetry, but I only like 'Jabberwoky.'"

This wasn't true—she also liked the work of Tennyson and Donne, whereas I was interested in more contemporary material. The one poem we agreed on was "Living in Sin" by Adrienne Rich, though Sophie seemed depressed by the honest portrayal of cohabitation. She must've sensed something tragic in the poem that would later manifest when we moved in together.

We'd agreed to transfer to the same university in the city. It made sense that we'd move in together, as things between us were "serious."

Our cohabitation was a nightmare. I was smoking and hiding it from her, not an easy feat in a one-bedroom apartment. She was used to being alone and often kicked me out of the apartment when she needed space or when she needed to defecate. She couldn't handle the idea that I was sitting in the next room while she voided her bowels.

I went on a lot of walks. Up Fullerton to Clark Street and as far south as Division if the weather was nice. Then back toward

Diversey, maybe all the way to Belmont before coming back to see if I was permitted reentry to our little love nest. Sophie often wondered why I was gone so long. She'd missed me. What was I doing? Where had I been?

"You asked me to leave for a while."

"Not for that long."

"Well, how long next time?"

"If I have to tell you, it's ruined."

These were the days before cell phones. There was no way to reach me when I went out for my little constitutionals. If we'd been a couple in the early 21st century, she would've surely sent me text after text chastising me for wandering so far from the apartment.

Some nights I went to the diner. It was open all night, smoking was permitted, and a cup of coffee could be nursed for a half hour or so. Then a refill, then another, then it was time to go. The waitress was nice enough to let me stay without concern for the lack of tips she was making on my meager check. And the cigarette smoke that I reeked of could easily be blamed on the other patrons.

"I sat in the nonsmoking section, but you know how smoke travels."

When I went to the diner to give Sophie her goddamn space, I would, of course, bring a book. At that time, I was reading a lot of Henry Miller. I can't say I was enjoying his fiction, which felt designed solely to cultivate his own myth, though phrases like "We went into a blind fuck" are certainly memorable.

Sophie and I officially called it quits after a blow up in the apartment. She'd had enough of my behavior—rightly so! I was a bad boyfriend. I went out a lot and when I was home, we fought. That day was no different; I can't recall exactly what we were fighting about, but it got ugly. Lots of regrettable words were exchanged. I said something vile enough to cause her to throw a book at my head. I ducked in time to avoid a flying *Plexus*, the weightiest Henry Miller book, which hit the wall and chipped off some paint and a chunk of our security deposit.

A week later, all traces of Sophie were gone. She took everything: the bed, the phone, the dresser, even the toilet paper. I was left with a love seat to sleep on, one bowl, one fork, one spoon, and my coffee mug with an illustration of Kurt Vonnegut's face. I bought cans of soup, then had to ask a neighbor to lend me her can opener when I remembered that Sophie took ours with her.

Despite the Spartan conditions, that was one of the happiest months of my life. I had no TV, so I read a lot of books. My radio only tuned in a few channels, mostly the classical stations, and I had only a few CDs to play. The soundtrack to my month alone was made up of Shubert, Charles Mingus, and John Zorn. I finished William S. Burroughs's *Junky* in a few hours, then read *Queer*, then thought that maybe I'd hibernated enough. A few steps outside, a trip to the diner, then to the bar and very soon I found friends. But I immediately wanted to be back in my cave. I thanked my pals for the drink they'd just bought me, went back home and started reading *The Castle*.

Later that night, Kafka on my chest, I saw a cockroach on the wall across from me. It wasn't moving, and I probably could've killed it, but I was too lazy. *Maybe he's like me, just hanging out, doing his thing, just trying to get some quiet*, I thought.

"Is that what's going on here? Are you just doing your thing? Minding your own business?"

The roach didn't answer.

"Maybe you're out on your ass. Got kicked out by the little woman."

Silence.

"Mine left me. It's okay, though. We weren't good for each other. Anyway, I'm an asshole."

Quiet.

"You could disagree, you know. Tell me I'm not so bad."

No words.

"Fine. It's true—I'm an asshole. I'm actually a lot happier now that she's gone. Really. I know that's what people say after a break up, but it's true. I'm enjoying myself immensely. This is the life, let me tell you. Laying around, drinking when I want, smoking indoors. Reading, listening to music. We got it pretty good here. If your lady kicked you out, be happy. You could be in a worse situation."

The roach remained silent.

"I mean, you could be dead. We both could be."

Nothing.

"Okay, goodnight." I said. "If you're here in the morning, I'll kill you."

I fell asleep, woke up hours later with a sore back and a dry mouth, scratched myself and looked for the roach. He was gone.

My Drinking part 2

August 2016, Chicago, IL

In order to better gauge the severity of my drinking, I've decided to self-diagnose using the AUDIT (Alcohol Use Disorders Identification Test). This handy questionnaire is available for free to anyone with access to the internet, though I'm including the questions here so that they might provide readers with a chance for immediate reflection. I'm adding my commentary at no additional cost.

1. *How often do you have a drink containing alcohol?*
   a. Never
   b. Monthly or less
   c. 2-4 times a month
   d. 2-3 times a week
   e. 4 or more times a week

Obviously not never, certainly more than monthly, and more than four times a week. But I fail to see the point of this question. Anyone driven to taking this test is likely to answer "4 or more times a week," so right out of the gate the respondent feels judged. Nice going, AUDIT. Way to make a guy run to the bar.

2. *How many drinks containing alcohol do you have on a typical day when you are drinking?*
   a. 1-2
   b. 3-4
   c. 5-6

> *d. 7-9*
>
> *e. 10 or more*

Well, it's hard to say, exactly. What's a typical day? I mean, some days it's one or two and some it's three or four, though I'm not against five or six depending on the day. I mean, if you had days like mine—like last month when I graded twenty student papers... AUDIT, you'd certainly have downed three or four, if not five or six. And what about weddings? An open bar is an invite for three, at least. Any less and you're insulting the bride and groom.

> 3. *How often do you have six or more drinks on one occasion?*
>   *a. Never*
>   *b. Less than Monthly*
>   *c. Monthly*
>   *d. Weekly*
>   *e. Daily or almost daily*

Oh, I don't know. Less than monthly, though who's counting? Anyway, math makes me break out in binge drinking.

> 4. *How often during the last year did you find that you were not able to stop drinking once you had started?*
>   *a. Never*
>   *b. Less than Monthly*
>   *c. Monthly*
>   *d. Weekly*
>   *e. Daily or almost daily*

I've not really stopped since starting. I stop for the night and sleep and wake up and eat and work and then maybe I'll start again, but stopping completely? Stopping philosophically? What exactly do you mean, AUDIT?

> 5. *How often during the last year have you failed to do what was normally expected of you because of drinking?*
>   *a. Never*

b. Less than Monthly

c. Monthly

d. Weekly

e. Daily or almost daily

Each day I fail, but it has nothing to do with alcohol.

6. *How often during the last year have you needed a first drink in the morning to get yourself going after a heavy drinking session?*

   a. Never

   b. Less than Monthly

   c. Monthly

   d. Weekly

   e. Daily or almost daily

I can't remember, but if I could, I'd surely need a drink to forget.

7. *How often during the last year have you had a feeling of guilt or remorse after drinking?*

   a. Never

   b. Less than Monthly

   c. Monthly

   d. Weekly

   e. Daily or almost daily

365 days in a row, though please take my Catholic upbringing into consideration.

8. *How often during the last year have you been unable to remember what happened the night before because of drinking?*

   a. Never

   b. Less than Monthly

   c. Monthly

   d. Weekly

   e. Daily or almost daily

Sadly, never. If this question has told me anything, it's that I need to drink more.

9. *Have you or someone else been injured because of you drinking?*
   a. No
   b. Yes, but not in the last year
   c. Yes, during the last year

Physically, no, but emotionally? Actually… let's not explore this further.

10. *Has a relative, friend, doctor, or other health care worker been concerned about your drinking or suggested you cut down?*
    a. No
    b. Yes, but not in the last year
    c. Yes, during the last year

Yes, during the last year, and thanks for reminding me. It's nice to have so many people in my life who care. I feel loved. Well done, AUDIT. You ended on a good note.

While the resulting score of this test has indicated—rather annoyingly—that perhaps I should slow down, I'm inspired by AUDIT to create my own questionnaire regarding the amount of money, time, and energy taxed by bibliophilia.

Soft Lunacy Test
1. How often do you buy books you already own?
   a. Never
   b. Less than Monthly
   c. Monthly
   d. Weekly
   e. Daily or almost daily

2. How often do you badger book clerks about the condition of a book before you buy it?
   a. Never
   b. Less than Monthly
   c. Monthly

    d. Weekly

    e. Daily or almost daily

3. Have you ever bought a book in a language you cannot read because you like the book so much you want a copy in a foreign tongue?

    a. Never

    b. Yes, but not in the last year

    c. Yes, during the last year

    d. Yes, what's your point?

4. Have you ever bought a book you already own because you saw a cover that was different than the one you have at home?

    a. Never

    b. Yes, but not in the last year

    c. Yes, during the last year

    d. Yes…. And?

5. Have you ever lied about owning a book because you didn't want to lend it to a friend?

    a. Never

    b. Yes, but the friend was not to be trusted with my precious book

6. Do you categorize books as "reading copies" versus "shelf copies"?

    a. No, who would do such a thing?

    b. Of course. I'm not going to write on the pages of a nice hardback when I can annotate a cheap paperback copy

7. Do you organize your home library by publisher, genre, or geographical region (i.e. a Latin American, Balkan, South Asian section)?
   a. No, that sounds like work
   b. Yes, but I'm thinking of reorganizing them again

8. Have you ever held onto a book that you don't like simply because you may want to try to read it again in the future?
   a. No, that's ridiculous, my tastes won't change
   b. Yes, but only for a year and then I got rid of it
   c. Yes, but I've not gotten around to trying to read it again, maybe next year

9. Have you ever taken a large tome with you during a commute by bus, train, or airplane, even though you knew doing so would cause discomfort?
   a. No, I bring a small book or Kindle
   b. Yes, but I regret it
   c. Yes, and I regret nothing

10. When you visit someone's home for the first time, do you judge them based on the books on their shelves?
    a. No, my friends don't read
    b. No, taste is relative
    c. Yes, but I know I'm being a prick
    d. Yes, rightly so

I'll not provide a score sheet for you to measure your bibliophilia. Chances are, you know just by answering how deep into the soft lunacy you reside.

The Problem With Multiple Interpretations

2006, Chicago, IL

Written on the Body. On the fucking body! What a great book. My book of love. The book I gave my wife when we started dating.

I'm cocky enough to take credit for passing my taste in literature to others. My wife read Jeanette Winterson because of me; I read Juan Rulfo because of her. We continue to influence each other. But Fern had no taste in anything when I met her. She didn't listen to music or read much, save for a few sci-fi books, and she liked movies but never really cared about any of them enough to have a favorite. They were mere distractions. After living with me for a few years, she grudgingly read Kurt Vonnegut. About a year after we split, she began reading Faulkner, who I'd long called the greatest American writer. I distinctly recall her looking at *As I Lay Dying* with understandable trepidation (Faulkner's genius is pretty intimidating) and moving on to the more familiar terrain of Orson Scott Card.

After we broke up, Fern told me how much she was enjoying Faulkner. And Vonnegut. And Murakami. And a lot of books I'd recommended over the years. Inspired by this newfound love of literature, she went back to school to study writing.

When Fern graduated with her BA, she threw herself a party at a local bar. I got an invitation. There was some idea that we'd remain friends post-relationship, or at least we'd maintain a level of civility. It wasn't an acrimonious split, but I wasn't interested in hanging out with her.

I went to the party anyway. A drink's a drink.

149

After some catching up chat with her mother and brother, I began my exit. Fern stopped me at the door.

"No present?"

It's true: I didn't buy her anything. No malice behind it, I just didn't think about getting her a gift.

"Well," I told her, "I already gave you your taste in literature."

She couldn't deny this.

After Fern and I were kaput, I met Cassandra. In hindsight, gifting her *Written on the Body* was a dick move. Giving someone a book is usually a nice thing, but I was essentially asking her to read the novel as a means of seduction, the way assholes make mix tapes for would-be romantic partners. Using someone else's art to charm a potential boy/girlfriend is a bit unoriginal. How many sweet young things have been wooed via cassettes full of The Velvet Underground, Peter Gabriel's "In Your Eyes" and Jeff Tweedy singing, "I'm trying to break your heart"?

In 2006, I met Winterson. She came to Chicago to promote her book *Lighthousekeeping*. I'd been writing record reviews for an online music magazine and had figured out how to interview musicians: find their managers, contact them, pretend you work for a big media outlet and ask for an interview.

I told Winterson's American agent that I was a writer for a Chicago publication called *New City*. I wasn't, though they have since published a few of my essays, so considering the odd nature of her books and the way she plays with time and space, in the Wintersonian sense I wasn't lying. Winterson consented to an interview at her hotel a few hours before she was scheduled to read for an audience. I was working for a law firm at the time and had to take an extra-long lunch break, which ended up being nearly three hours.

We entered the lobby of the hotel. (I couldn't meet Winterson without bringing Cassandra along.) I called up to Winterson's room and nervously told her I was supposed to interview her.

"Yes, you are," said my favorite living novelist. "Why not come up, then? There's all that piped in music down there. All those lights. It's distracting."

"Come up to your room?"

"Yes."

She gave me the number. I told Cassandra we were going up to Winterson's room, which seemed really big. Her *room!* Where she would sleep that night!

I'll likely never meet a friendlier writer. Winterson offered a handshake and, later, a hug, and was incredibly generous with her time. The conversation went on longer than it needed to for the purpose of an interview, but I didn't think of leaving until she politely told me that she had to get onto other things before the reading that night. I didn't get through any of my prepared questions, either. The conversation just sort of happened. Thankfully, I recorded it.

As we were leaving, I asked if she wouldn't mind signing some books. When we got to *Written on the Body*, I told her that I'd given that book to Cassandra, who, when not taking pictures, was standing star struck and watching the interview.

"I credit our relationship to your novel," I said.

Winterson signed it and wrote, *His book of love.*

I also asked her to sign *The Powerbook*. On the first page under her printed name, she wrote: "To Vincent. Write whatever you want." Earlier I'd told her that I wanted to be a writer but worried that no one would read any of my wayward prose pieces or oddball poems. Her response was touching, sincerely inspirational. I floated out of the room.

I showed the inscription to Cassandra.

"How do you know she didn't mean the interview?"

"Huh?"

"I mean," she said, "Winterson might've meant write whatever you want for the interview."

"Oh fuck. Like she meant it insultingly? Like 'You journalists make up anything you want anyway, so go ahead and write whatever'?"

"I don't know."

"I'm not even a fucking journalist," I said.

To this day, I don't exactly know how to interpret Winterson's message. I want to read it as encouraging, as if the mad woman of the modern novel was offering advice about staying true to my own vision, but for all I know she meant it derisively. That's the blessing and curse of literature: the possibility of multiple interpretations.

The Flophouse

1995, Chicago, IL

I was never one for drugs, not counting alcohol, tobacco, caffeine, and chocolate, which some consider mood altering, therefore a drug, though we can argue that if you like. When my roommates announced that they were planning to spend the night at a neighbor's house tripping on psilocybin mushrooms, I told them to have a good time and made my own plans for the evening, which included: a six pack of beer, a pack of cigarettes, a comfortable chair, a copy of *Locos: A Comedy of Gestures* by Felipe Alfau, and some peace and quiet.

Living with anyone is difficult. You have to make concessions, deal with their figurative and sometimes literal shit, and try to get along even though you will see them in their least agreeable guises. They will make noise when you want quiet and fall asleep when you want company. They will eat your leftovers and claim ignorance. They will borrow things without asking, clog the drain and forget to wash their dishes. You will also do every one of these things, so don't get high and mighty. Of course when you commit these sins of cohabitation you will likely have a good excuse, one your roomies will eternally lack.

Along with Carl the slob, I lived with three other young men in a three-bedroom apartment that was a year away from being condemned. The number of residents would swell to six before long, and then a few girlfriends started staying over with enough regularity to push the number of inhabitants of 2141 N. Southport Avenue into the double digits. We affectionately referred to the place as "the flophouse," a moniker that was meant to raise a smile, though, as is often the case with ironic jokes, the gag quickly stops being funny. It truly was a goddamn flophouse. People came and went. They slept on the floor, in the bathtub, wherever they could squeeze in. It was cramped, dirty, and smelled of smoke and spilled beer. We had a mouse at one point, a parade of centipedes, a toilet that periodically worked, and a kitchen sink complete with a faucet that offered only rusty water. It was freezing in the winter and sweltering in the summer. A real dump.

Even a dump can be beautiful. The way to make the flophouse something close to paradise was to remove the bodies. So, again, when the roomies decided to vacate in order to explore the boundaries of their consciousness or whatever, I was thrilled. *A night of solitude!*

There is apparently some quality I possess that is calming to the drug-addled mind. Friends liked having me around when they were on psychedelics. They knew I wasn't tripping, and that was a sort of anchor for them. As long as Vinny's around, someone's in control. That being the case, I shouldn't have been surprised when the phone rang not even an hour into my evening. I put *Locos* down and answered the call.

"Vinny?"

"Yeah?"

"It's Carl."

"Oh, hey."

"Hey!"

"Aren't you supposed to be tripping?"

"I am tripping!"

"Oh. Okay."

"I needed to call you. Man, why aren't you here?"

"I'm home," I said, which was a silly thing to say—after all, he'd called the apartment.

"I know. I, I… I needed to call."

He sounded out of his head, more at a loss for words than he normally was. I asked him why he was calling, and he mumbled a bit and started talking to others in the room.

"Carl, are you at the party."

"What party?"

"The mushroom party or whatever you guys were going to."

"Yeah, yeah! We're on drugs!"

"Okay."

"And I needed to call you."

"Why?"

"Because… Vinny, I've come to depend on you like a bitch."

From there Carl went into a speech about our recent differences, the Bob Dylan fist fight, the condom on the floor, all the grievances we'd supposedly put behind us. He apologized and told me I was a great guy, a true friend, and that, again, he had come to depend on me "like a bitch," a proclamation that generated laughter from him and the others in the room.

"That's very nice. Have fun tonight and be careful," I said.

"Wait, don't go!"

Carl needed me to be on the phone with him. I was his rock, the thing that would keep his head from going to a bad place.

"Dude, you should come over," he said, but I declined. I wasn't ready to abandon my private evening of reading and beer.

I agreed to remain on the phone for as long as Carl needed me. Two beers later, he was still babbling nonsense in my ear and intermittently talking to the others. I told him that it sounded like he was in a good place and maybe I ought to be going when he yelled, "Don't hang up!"

Cradling the phone against my shoulder, I went back to my book. Three hours later, I had most of *Locos* read. Carl had checked in on me while I read, and I had to stop for a bit and assure him that I was there, that everything was fine, he was fine, the universe was fine, but I managed to get through the book without much distraction. It was easy to tune out the drug-fueled conversation coming at me through the earpiece. Maybe if I'd picked a denser novel—something by Dostoevsky or Virginia Woolf or Thomas Pynchon—I'd have had less success, but I read the entirety of *Locos* in that position: reclining in the comfy chair, beer at my side, occasional cigarette, phone against my shoulder.

Finally, after nearly five hours, Carl let me go. I stood up and stretched. My neck was killing me. My back was stiff. My ear throbbed and I had a headache. But I was alone in the flophouse with *Locos* still in my thoughts and one beer left. I opened it, lit a cigarette, strolled around the flophouse and felt at peace.

The Wisdom of Dogs

September 2016, Chicago, IL

Someone said to me, "pets die" and that dealing with their passing is part of being a pet owner. It's hard, "but it's not like a person died."

It's no wonder I prefer the company of dogs.

Last week, a book arrived in the mail: *Falling Ill* the last poems of C. K. Williams. The book isn't slated for publication until early next year, but I got a galley copy to read and review.

The book was written as Williams was facing his death. Diagnosis dominates the early poems, then decay. It's not a glum collection, but it's not exactly the sort of reading I feel like doing. Too many people are dying in my city, in the world, in the news. It's been a death-heavy year and, though he is one of my favorite writers, I'm not in the mood to dive into C. K. Williams' meditations on his demise.

I first felt the lump in my balls two months ago. It seemed strange—I couldn't recall a third, smaller testicle being there before. *That's funny. Might want to see a doctor about this.*

Rather than make a doctor's appointment, I first went to Google to read a lot of confusing information, then read more information that contradicted the last set of information, then started feeling every symptom on the screen. *I'm dying. This is how it ends.*

For several weeks, I've obsessively thought about and inspected my balls. I wake up—it's the first thing I do. *Better make sure another lump hasn't formed.* I ride the subway and look at all the men and wonder if they have a lump on their balls, if this is just something that just happens when we age. Increased chance of heart trouble, swelling prostate, lumpy testicles. The only relief from thoughts of testicular cancer comes during class time when I stand in front of students and try to get them to put their smartphones away long enough to discuss the essays they didn't read. Then it's back to my office where I have to grade papers, though what's the point if I'm going to die soon? This thought allows me to skip work and go out for tea or a sandwich or a lot of chocolate and then home for a drink. Life's too short to deny ourselves simple indulgences, especially when we're walking around with lumps on our private bits.

Update: Today I learned that I don't have cancer. My urologist told me so after asking me to drop my pants, lie back, relax. I managed all but the relaxing. For a brief duration of time that seemed interminable, he manipulated my scrotum. After apologizing for "going to town" on my testicles, he assured me the lumps are not tumors. An ultrasound is scheduled to make sure, but I left the doctor with a renewed skip in my step, thrilled that I won't have to endure the pain of medical treatment, at least not at this time.

To celebrate not having testicular cancer, I agreed to meet Cassandra for dinner at the Red Lion Pub. On my way there, I stopped at the grocery store for a bottle of whiskey. My logic: if I have booze to drink at home, I'll drink less at the bar. Saves money!

The line at the grocery store was rather long. Ahead of me, an elderly woman struggled with the self-check-out technology that has grown where once cashiers stood.

"How do I do this?" she asked. "I don't know my pin number!"

The attendant patiently helped her while I stood fuming over the delay.

Once the old woman finished her transaction and shuffled off, I rushed to the self-check-out. It didn't take long to realize that a pile of fecal matter was on the floor, but I sadly noticed too late to avoid stepping in it.

"What the fuck?" I asked aloud, then apologized to the man behind me who was covering the ears of a small child. The attendant asked, "What's the matter," and I cautioned her from making the mistake I'd made.

"Oh no, she didn't?" asked the attendant.

"She did," I replied, then demanded that I be shown to the bathroom. Rather than escort me there, I was given directions which were, thankfully, easy to follow. Then I placed the shoe under the faucet and waved my hand to engage the motion sensor mechanism that released a stream of water with frequent interruptions. The water did its best to remove the shit from the bottom of my shoe and soon, with the help of the hand dryer, I left with a mostly clean pair of footwear.

I got to the bar before my wife. The bartender saw my face and asked if everything was okay. I asked for a double Jameson and a Guinness.

"Sure thing. Are you eating tonight?"

"Maybe never again."

I'm able to laugh at the nasty experience, but I was disgusted at the time, and while I did manage to eat (after quite a bit of drinking) I'm unable to forget the sight of that pile of excrement on the off-white floor of the grocery store. That poor woman—so confused, barely able to walk, just trying to buy some milk and bread before returning to whatever nightmare she calls home. Her body is barely her own anymore.

I'd not be surprised to learn that this woman has an otherwise fulfilling life with people who love her and activities to occupy her and a real sense of purpose, but at that moment—standing in a store, unsure of how to pay for food, unable to control her bowels—she was an undignified creature the rest of us were trying to avoid, a source of frustration to the employee who had no choice but deal with her. Not a human being; a conflict.

I suppose our tenacity, our unwillingness to give up, is what makes us beautiful, even at our most repulsive. We go on. Despite humiliation, pain, and fear, we keep going. In the end, we're all animals fighting out of instinct. Beckett wrote: "I can't go on. I'll go on," ending his book *L'Innommable* with those words that perfectly sum up the human condition. We're decaying, dying, falling apart slowly, and yet enduring. In the face of certain death, we keep going.

Unlike other species, we have foreknowledge of our coming demise. Animals don't think about their deaths, or so I assume. They just go on, like Beckett's creation, until they don't. In the days before my dog died, we walked the same streets we'd walked for years. He relieved himself. He ate food. He slept. He played with his toys. He licked my face. He lived. He didn't dwell on mortality the way I do. He was smarter than I'll ever be.

I, Asshole

October 2016, Skokie, IL

Today, while shopping with Cassandra, I noticed that the cashier—a young woman with those inexplicable devices that stretch the earlobes into grotesque holes—had letters tattooed on each finger that spelled: CATS MEOW. My wife commented favorably on the tattoo. The young woman thanked her. The exchange was pleasant, but I had to ruin it by pointing out that the tattoo was missing an apostrophe.

"Well, I was a finger short," she said. Immediately I looked for a place to add the punctuation mark. The webbing between the fingers seemed the logical spot, but I left it alone. For a minute. Then I tried to spin my observation by pointing out that perhaps her intention was to make a declarative statement: Cats meow. Indeed they do!

Cassandra told me I was making things worse, a euphemistic way of telling me to shut the fuck up.

We left the store, Cassandra the owner of some new lipstick and I in possession of the knowledge that I am, indeed, an asshole.

While far from a perfect grammarian, I insist that CAT'S MEOW include the apostrophe, lest CAT'S, possessive, become CATS plural. I said as much to Cassandra who rolled her eyes.

"It's a small but crucial punctuation mark," I said. "What might we lose if we eschew it? What happens when we let the loose grammatical rules of text messages and the hieroglyphics of emojis hold sway?"

"You spend enough time grading papers," Cassandra said. "Why are you grading tattoos?"

She's right, of course. Only an asshole cares that much about an apostrophe. But at least I'm an asshole who knows damn well how to punctuate CAT'S MEOW.

How Not to Move a Library

2000, Chicago, IL – Asheville, NC – Chicago, IL

The months before I pulled up stakes for Dixie were difficult. I was pushing thirty, working in an office where I made barely enough to cover rent, and living with Fern. I no longer felt anything for her that might be confused with affection. It was mutual. We'd been together for a few unhappy years, having stayed together out of habit, both of us being lazy people evident in the length of our unsatisfying relationship and the width of our waistbands. We used unhealthy distractions to keep our unhealthy relationship going for as long as we could, but in the summer of 2000 it all went south. So I decided to do the same. To Asheville, North Carolina, specifically.

Why did our relationship go south? Fern had stopped flirting with my friends via email, but her interest in seeing other people hadn't diminished. She didn't act on that interest, partially because she wasn't able to. Her would-be paramour rejected her. She told me about the incident, her spurned overtures to the young lad—an angry young man who worked at a bookstore (she sure had a type)—and sought some sort of comfort from me. I wasn't angry that she'd been flirting with another man. I'd accepted that she was looking elsewhere and was partially happy to have her off my back, but that she thought I would lend a sympathetic ear was too much.

"I'm sorry you got the Heisman."

"The what?"

"The Heisman. As in the Heisman Trophy."

"What the hell are you talking about?"

163

"The trophy for college football. It looks like someone putting their hand up and saying 'Stop.' It's what my friends used to call getting rejected."

"You're an asshole."

We fought long and hard enough to reach the mutual decision that it was time to end the farce. We agreed to break up.

Why Asheville? Why the hell not? A beautiful town nestled in the Blue Ridge mountains, cheap rent, plenty of good places to eat, friendly people, weird hippie vibe with a dash of Harley Davidson culture to give the city some edge—it seemed as good a place as any. And I knew someone who lived there: D.C., who convinced me to move sight unseen.

I had to consider the weight of the decision. I was a lifelong Midwesterner, born and raised in the south suburbs of Chicago. I had no idea what southern living would be like. I had no job prospects in Asheville. All I had were some books that I refused to sell and some old, well-worn clothing.

I batted the idea around and asked friends for advice. Most of them had little to say, save for one pal who offered this: "Sometimes it's good to shake your life up, turn it upside-down and see what breaks and what sticks." Something of a messy metaphor, and maybe the worst advice I've ever heard, but it made sense at that moment. *Fuck it*, I thought. *I'm moving.*

Quitting my job was easy. Since starting at the Metropolitan Healthcare Council, I'd switched departments three times and realized that no one stayed in any one position long enough for their supervisor to give a damn, so when I told mine I was leaving at the end of the month she smiled, asked a few perfunctory questions about where I was off to, called me by the wrong name and wished me well.

Despite being broken up, Fern and I stayed in the apartment. It was too early for her to move into her new residence. I had no friends in town to stay with—all of them had either left Chicago or stopped taking my calls. I couldn't face my family. My mom wasn't happy about my plan to relocate 660 miles away, my brother was busy with his own toxic relationship, and I was growing tired of answering my aunts, uncles, and cousins when they asked, "Why North Carolina?" And I'd already paid rent on the apartment. I couldn't afford to move elsewhere for the month, and I was too proud to sleep on my mom's couch, so I decided to be civil and stay with Fern until it was time to move.

We did our best to create a normal environment, and while we managed to stop yelling at each other, things were tense. Weirdly, I preferred the fights to the fake pleasantries. The tip-toeing ended after a few weeks of "How was work?" and "I'm thinking of ordering a pizza, do you want some?" and "Are you going to use the shower now? Oh no, it's okay. I can wait 'til you're done." I'd been sleeping on the couch since we broke up. Most of the time, I kept the area organized, but one morning I overslept and left for work without folding the blanket, fluffing the pillow and making the tiny living room look presentable. I got home and found a note reminding me that we both still shared the apartment and keeping it tidy was our mutual responsibility. I scribbled a hasty "Fuck you" under her pen marks and went for a walk.

Three hours at the Red Lion Pub seemed long enough—I walked back to the apartment. Fern was asleep. I took my place on the couch and tried to get some rest. I'm not sure how long I was out, but I woke confused. It was still dark. Someone was in the room with me.

"Are you up?"

She was sitting on the chair across from the couch.

"What are you doing here?"

"Couldn't sleep. Thought I might read or something."

"In the dark?"

She ignored that.

"I saw your note," she said.

"Yeah?"

"It was mean."

"Oh, stop it. We've been trying so hard, but let's just cut the shit."

"Why are talking to me like this? Don't you care about me at all?"

"I don't know... maybe this was a bad idea."

"It's a little late. You're leaving town."

"I meant us staying here for the month. That was a bad idea."

"Oh."

She may have been hurt, but it was dark and hard to see her face. I felt bad. Both of us contributed to the rotting of our relationship, but at that moment I felt entirely to blame.

Was that why I let her sit next to me? Or was I hurt and lonely? Or just stupid? Stupid enough to let her curl up with me and then—dumb, dumb—kiss me. And then...

I don't care to go into further detail.

In the morning I felt rotten. Hungover, full of regret, I showered and left for work before she woke. The rest of the week I spent my nights walking through the city, visiting cafés and bars and diners, only coming home when I knew Fern would be asleep. I'd curl up on the couch and get a few hours rest before she woke me. Her movements in the apartment were loud and seemed deliberate, though I knew better than to complain or even to admit that I was awake. The smart thing was to keep my eyes closed and feign sleep. Eventually Fern would leave for her morning shift and I'd get up, shower, make coffee, and enjoy my solitude.

We managed to go on like that until it was time to move out. Our landlord had decided to keep most of the security deposit. I knew little of tenant's rights at the time and made no protestation about the lost money. Truly I was in a hurry to get out and didn't care about anything else.

Moving is difficult enough without adding arguments and accusations. We couldn't stop bickering. Little things were made large. I left the door open and a fly entered the apartment.

"I'm staying here a few more days. You don't have to let bugs in!"

She drank a bottle of water that I'd been saving, so I called her selfish. That sort of thing. For hours.

After my clothes were moved and most of the furniture was lugged to the alley, I had the last of my library to transport. I'd returned the rental van, which I'd used to haul most of the books to the post office. I'd reunite with them in a few days in North Carolina. I'd moved a few other boxes to my mom's house the week before. My plan was to leave them at my mother's where they'd stay until I had the money to send her, so she could have them shipped. But a few bags remained. Total: four grocery bags filled with pocket paperbacks, not a lot considering the entirety of the library, but enough to miss. And I do miss them, for they were sacrificed after I tried carrying all four bags at once to a taxi on Southport Avenue. When the bottom of one of the bags fell out, and a pile of paperbacks spilled onto the street, I swear I heard Fern chuckle.

I lost it.

"Motherfucker!" I said, then dropped the other bags, kicked them and their contents a few times, and got in the cab.

"Just go," I told the driver.

I didn't look back, but I like to think Fern wore a confused stare as the taxi drove away. A great last impression of her ex.

The idea that a chunk of my library was left scattered across Southport infuriates me now. I have no idea what books were in those bags, though I probably lost a copy of *Mrs. Dalloway* and I can't seem to locate my Gore Vidal novels. It's hard to miss what you can't even name, but I miss those books anyway. I miss the idea of them. Still, considering I've lived in four different apartments on Southport Avenue, it seems that the road deserved to have some part of me left on it, like pouring a bit of liquor on the curb for those who have passed from this world. Keep looking down on me, old books, and I'll keep my head up. Peace, homies.

Travel on the cheap consisted of flying from Chicago to Raleigh, North Carolina, getting picked up there and transported to a Metra train to Charlotte and then driven to Asheville. So, a plane, a train, and an automobile. Because things worked out great in that movie with a similar name.

I got a ride to the airport from my mom and stepdad. My mother cried as I was leaving. Great—I'd made two women cry in the last few weeks, one of them I still cared for. I thought of my mother's tears during the entire plane ride. *What kind of son makes his mom cry?*

When I landed in Raleigh, I felt lost. I had a friend there, Dusty, who agreed to pick me up and show me around me until it was time to board the train. In our little group of pretentious assholes, mediocre students, and would-be nihilists, Dusty was known for his ability to polish off a half pint of vodka in the time it took Tom Waits to sing "I Don't Wanna Grow Up" (two minutes and thirty-two seconds). Dusty's easy handling of booze and weed made his foray into harder drugs inevitable. In retrospect, some friendly advice to keep the intake of toxins at a minimum might've gone far and prevented a lot of legal and financial trouble for the guy, but who among us in those hazy college days was about to stop anyone from fucking their life up?

Thirty-seven minutes late, Dusty pulled up in his 1969 Ford Fairlane. I hadn't seen him since he moved back to North Carolina five years prior. I was worried he wasn't going to show, remembering on the plane ride that, though a fun guy to have at a party, he wasn't the most responsible individual. Maybe I should've called a taxi. But there he was, charmingly disheveled with a sloppy grin and Run DMC on the stereo. Dusty got out of the car, hugged me, and jumped back into the driver's seat. I suspected he'd had a wild night and maybe was riding on last night's energy, but I know now that part of his lively and erratic behavior was the result of cocaine. I was too tired to care about his haphazard way of changing lanes or tendency to stop on a dime whenever he decided to show me a landmark, even as we nearly hit a few pedestrians.

"See that?"

I answered in the affirmative.

"That's where I got laid the first time."

"Wow. That ought to be on the town's list of notable tourist attractions."

Dusty laughed, drove us further into town, showed me a few more of his favorite Raleigh spots, then schooled me in the ways of the south.

"First thing to keep in mind: the rules for buying liquor 'round here are different. In Chicago, you can buy alcohol whenever you want, right? Here they stop sales at certain times depending on the day of the week. Sundays are dry in some counties. So, make sure you know the hours, or do what I do and never let your home bar go unstocked."

"Home bar?"

"Yep. Load up on beer in the fridge and a few bottles of whatever you like. I keep a few fifths of vodka at home. And a few pints for emergencies. Keep 'em in the kitchen, right on the counter. You can see your reserves that way. You'll never be left dry on Sunday."

"Okay."

"Now, there's a special kind of insanity in the south that's different from what you're used to. Northern insanity is like people walking the streets all fucked up and weird. Homeless people who got all messed up by the big cruel city. And a lot of belligerence. There's not so much of that down here. People're mostly nice, even the weirdoes, and there's not a lot of homeless. But southern insanity is its own breed. I knew a guy used to work for my dad. He was as close to homeless as you can get. Lived in some halfway house or something. Worked as a day laborer. He was sitting in my living room waiting to go to work rehabbing one of my dad's properties when he says, 'I shit my pants. I can't work today.' And he was telling the truth. He shit himself. I'm not sure if he did it because he couldn't help it or if he was just trying to get out of a day of work, but he definitely shit himself."

"Couldn't he have just called in sick?"

"That's southern insanity for you. Rather than lie or risk offending your boss with some tale about being sick, you show up with shit in your pants so they'll send you home."

We found a small eatery and feasted on fattening southern cuisine and sweet tea. Then we went for drinks at a bar across from the train station. I nearly missed the train—there was no clock in the bar and we were both too busy kicking around old stories and downing pints of lager. I made it with hardly a minute to spare, hugged my old friend, and told him I'd keep in touch. That was sixteen years ago. I've not seen him since.

The train ride was long, and my stomach was a mess of beer and fried food. I tried to read but couldn't concentrate. Young men surrounded me, all busy using words like "faggot," all tall and blonde and too athletic to make me want to challenge them. At one point they started tossing a football across aisles and over the heads of the rest of us who were stationary out of fear of taking a pigskin to the nose.

When the Charlotte stop came at last, I dashed off the train and looked for D.C. to rescue me. He was there on time, thankfully, and escorted me to his mom's house, an old two-story on the outskirts of town.

"Is there a phone I can use?" I asked.

"Long distance?"

"Yeah. Sorry."

I'd promised Fern that I'd call her when I got to North Carolina. I don't know why—we were barely speaking when I left, but she'd insisted, and I'd agreed.

She was crying. No build up, just tears from the second she picked up until the second I hung up. Between those seconds was the most awkward conversation imaginable. She cried, apologized, said she was wrong to have kicked me out. (*"Kicked me out?"* Is that what happened?") I didn't know what to say. I wasn't used to women being sad when I leave. Not sure what else to do, I hung up.

A few minutes later, the phone rang. *Fuck*—caller ID. I told her that it was late, that I'd been travelling all day, that D.C. was letting me crash at his mom's house, that his mom was sleeping and that the phone was waking her. Fern didn't care. She wanted to talk. I told her I'd call her later in the week when I got set up in Asheville. I wished her a good night.

A few minutes passed before the phone rang again.

"Jesus, you have to stop calling. It's late!"

"Don't yell at me!"

We managed to mutually calm down and end the conversation on a somewhat civil note, but I had to swear I'd call her the next day.

"Pretty short leash there, Vinny."

"Don't start," I said.

"Didn't you break up?"

"Yeah."

"And she's still calling? And you're still taking the calls?"

"I don't want to talk about it."

We watched a movie and I drank a few beers with D.C. until I could no longer keep my eyes focused. I woke on the couch, confused and sore. Weeks of couch sleeping were taking their toll.

"This place in Asheville, is there a bed for me?"

"Well..."

That meant no. D.C. had a bed, but I would have to find one for myself. I never did. The best I managed was an air mattress the last tenant left in the garage. Years of smoking made blowing it up a chore, and in the end, I opted for the more comfortable option: the living room couch.

"You should get a bed. I mean, once you get a job," said D.C.

"I think it's my destiny to forever sleep on couches."

My books arrived a few days later. I unpacked the boxes and stacked the contents along the wall of my room. Aside from the books, I had very little: just a pile of clothes and a half-filled air mattress. The room, according to D.C., was soulless.

"A mess," he said. "A soulless mess."

"Cicero said that a room without books is like a body without a soul. I have books."

"But no furniture. We need to get you some furniture."

I had no intention of spending money, so I made do with the meager accommodations, assuring D.C. that I'd manage just fine. He was making good money as a school counselor and could afford luxuries like a VCR and TV, both of which he told me I was free to use. He may have hinted that I kick in for cable, but I ignored his request, not sure how I'd even pay for food.

"If you're looking to get over your breakup, you're kinda fucked," D.C. said.

"What?"

"There're no girls here to meet."

"None?"

"Well, there are, but they're either lesbians or they've slept with Johnny," he said referring to a mutual friend. Johnny lived in Asheville after moving from Chicago and had, apparently, taken the town by storm. An art school dropout with talent to burn and abundant good looks, Johnny had spent a few sex-and-drug-filled years in Asheville before moving on to some other small town to start a new protracted bacchanal.

"I'm not looking to meet anyone. And I wouldn't care if they'd slept with Johnny anyway."

"You sure? That guy got around."

I liked Asheville right off. The town has a laid-back feel and was full of vegan cafés where the food actually tasted like barbeque. The people were friendly, though a lot of them seemed like the types to drop out of society and start a commune, which is perhaps how the town was formed. I was a late comer to the new age collective, and while I tend to dislike concentrated hippie culture, I was nevertheless confident that I might blend in and—who knows?—get fully indoctrinated. I saw myself with long hair, poncho, and beads within a year. And the town had some nice bookshops. Asheville was especially proud of its native son Thomas Wolfe, though, considering the way he wrote about Asheville, which resulted in a sort of exile, I'm not sure why.

D.C. insisted we attend a party some of his new friends were throwing. Aside from not really knowing the partygoers (always awkward) I was clearly older than most of them. D.C. was a few years my junior, but his new pals seemed even younger. They shared the sort of familiarity that comes from time spent together and swapped stories of past teachers, road trips, and football games that further distanced me. I wanted to go back to the lousy room with the air mattress and read in quiet, but D.C. was determined that we start mixing into Asheville's social scene, such as it was.

Mix I did. The hippie kids were welcoming enough—one even offered me a beer upgrade from Pabst to Sam Adams. So why did I feel so out of place? The answer can only be that I was being an asshole. It's like the old rule of poker: if you look around the table and can't tell who the sucker is, you'd better look in the mirror.

"It's like you're setting up every conversation to fail," D.C. said.

"Huh?"

"You can't just introduce yourself like a normal person. You have to say, 'Hi, I'm Vince. What's your story?'"

"What's wrong with that?"

"It's confrontational."

"Just making conversation," I said.

"You bring that Chicago attitude with you."

"What Chicago attitude?"

"Like coming from a big city makes you above everyone."

"I don't think that! I like Asheville. Anyway, why do you think I moved here?"

He didn't answer.

Aside from these little tensions, I was getting along with D.C. well enough. In little time I got a sense of the town. Downtown Asheville is small enough to navigate without much trouble. And I had a surprising amount of job opportunities. After acing a Microsoft Office skills test—years of working in offices allowed me to pick up considerable software proficiency—a temp agency sent me to an interview on the other side of town. I had to take a bus there, not recommended in a city where every functional citizen drives. The rest of us nonfunctional citizens rode the bus trying hard not to make eye contact with the weirdo across from us. And, clad in fading chinos and an ill-fitting shirt with sweat stains under the armpits (Asheville mass transit offered no air conditioning), I was every bit as weird as the other weirdoes on the bus. Even the jittery junkies seemed to regard me with suspicion.

After exiting the bus, leaving the meth addicts and refugees from leper colonies to their commutes, I walked in the unforgiving southern heat to the tiny warehouse where I was to meet my future employer. He looked more than a bit like Sheriff Lobo and explained the job in the following way:

"You sit your ass at a desk and enter stuff into a computer from eight to four. Half hour lunch. No personal calls."

"Sounds good."

"Last guy left to be a Buncombe County deputy."

I was certain he said "Bumpkin County" but knew better than to ask.

"That's nice."

"Alright," he said. "Come on by tomorrow. We'll start you off."

My stint as a data entry goon in Asheville lasted only a few days despite being told that I was a valued asset to the company. I believed it—no one else there wanted to work. I wasn't in love with the job either, but I'd spent a few years working in offices and didn't really mind brainless tasks so long as I could listen to music on my headphones. And my small wage, the same as I was used to making in Chicago, was going to go considerably further in Asheville. I spent my time at the computer entering numbers into a database and dreaming of all the stuff I was going to buy with my first check.

But I couldn't stop thinking about the women I'd made cry. I called my mother a few times, always trying to make small talk, but the conversations were stilted. And then there was Fern. She'd kept up her habit of calling me to cry and yell and make me feel genuinely rotten. I might've gotten over that, but there was no avoiding the sense of responsibility I felt when she informed me that she was pregnant.

That night, that stupid night. Ugh. Look what happened. Dumb, dumb, dumb.

When I told D.C. I was moving back to Chicago, he didn't seem very surprised. In the three weeks I'd spent in Asheville we'd had a few discussions centered on what he perceived to be my lack of commitment to the arrangement. I'd made no effort to decorate the apartment or "make myself at home" and had, as he put it, "one foot out the door" the whole time. I disagreed, but what was the point of debating the matter? All I could do was apologize and try to explain to him that I had no choice but to go back. But I couldn't tell him why. I'd made a huge mistake, but the idea of telling anyone the truth seemed impossible. They'd find out soon enough, but in the meantime, I had to go back and sort myself out. I had to figure out what to do about Fern. Move back in with her and try to start a family? Send her money and live alone? I had no idea what the right play was, but I knew it involved going back and facing whatever waited.

I had only enough money for a Greyhound bus, the cheapest and least comfortable way to get from Asheville to Chicago. D.C. drove me to the station and waited with me until the bus arrived. Next to us was a box of used children's shoes for sale and a pile of chicken bones picked clean. No one in the station looked happy. Chances are if you're riding a Greyhound bus you fucked up somewhere along the way.

We joked a bit and seemed to be on good terms, but I felt shitty about leaving. D.C. now had to find someone to take over my room and help with the bills. We were supposed to be starting an adventure together in a new city. He said he understood, but I knew he was upset. I'm always disappointing someone.

My bus left at 9:30 PM and was scheduled to arrive in Chicago at

11:00 the next morning. An overnight trek through the south to the Midwest meant changing buses in Knoxville and again in Cincinnati and once more in Indianapolis. Between stops, I tried to sleep when not feeling the jerk of the bus changing lanes or exiting one highway for another. The people on the bus were all quiet. We rode together in a heavy silence. And I hated the silence. In it, there was no escape from the mocking voice that told me that I was going to be a father.

Changing buses meant I had to claim the books I'd packed in oversized gym bags and lug them from one bus to the next. Most of the library had been repacked in boxes and shipped to my mother's house in the suburbs, but to save money I'd stuffed the gym bags for travel with me back to Chicago. At the last bus change in Indiana, I felt the straps of one of the gym bags start to give and was sure I was about to repeat the incident from a few weeks prior when my books were sacrificed to Southport Avenue. I dropped the entire bag, hoisted the other into the storage bay at the bottom of the bus, and then carefully placed the failing gym bag alongside its more resilient twin. When I got to Chicago—blurry eyed and frantic—I collected both bags and dragged them outside to Harrison Street where my brother waited in his car ready to take me to our mother's house.

That night, my mother and stepdad took me to dinner. It was awkward. They were letting me stay with them. They said I could stay as long as I liked, but I knew they wanted me to figure out what I was doing. I was past the age where I could justifiably be a slacker.

"Thirty is when people take you seriously," my stepfather once told me. And I was going to be thirty in a less than a year. No career, no ambitions, just a pile of books I collected for some reason. And a pregnant ex-girlfriend.

I called her after dinner. Fern cried during the entire call. I was so sick of her goddamn tears.

We made arrangements to meet. I was planning to go to the city the next morning and start looking for a job. We'd have lunch if there was time, I told her. But the next afternoon, while I was supposed to be calling her to arrange a place to meet, I was in the middle of a room full of computers and soon-to-be-antiquated technology taking another office skills aptitude test. The employment recruiter said she could get me an interview that day. An hour later, I was in the lobby of a law firm waiting to be interviewed. I used a courtesy phone to call Fern and tell her I wouldn't make it to lunch, hanging up before she could protest.

The human resources manager asked basic questions about my experience.

"Do you know anything about working in a law firm?" she asked.

"Not really, but I'm a fast learner."

Whether or not she believed me, she decided that I should meet one of the lawyers. Frank Cahill, the most junior of partners at the firm, stepped into the room. He had a very south suburban Chicago accent and walked with swagger. Chewing on the arm of his glasses, he looked over my resume. He asked about my high school, then laughed a little. I didn't know what to make of that, but I left it alone. Then he put his glasses on and looked me over.

"You seem like a nice guy."

"Thanks."

"Alright. We'll let you know."

The next day, the human resources manager called to tell me I was hired.

My job was simple: I was to file claims against asbestos companies on behalf of pipe fitters and other construction workers, not to mention their wives and kids, many of whom had developed asbestos related diseases due to exposure. Perhaps the worst story I heard is that of a young woman who was dying from mesothelioma because her father had a habit of coming home from work and bouncing his little girl on his knee and hugging her close while still in asbestos dust covered work clothes. Stories like that bothered me a lot, but the job was easy. The pay was meager, but a steady check was what I most needed. I was on my way to being a responsible, gainfully employed man.

I moved back in with Fern. It seemed the right thing to do.

Less than a week into our new cohabitation, she told me she wasn't pregnant. I pressed her to explain, but she just said it was a false alarm. To this day I'm convinced she lied about the whole thing to get me to come back to Chicago, but admitting as much makes me feel like an arrogant prick. I'm not so goddamn special that she *had* to be with me. I was hardly what anyone would call a hot prospect. No money, no direction, no future. Still, I can't help but wonder what really happened. There are only three options I can imagine, none of them good.

A voice in my head told me that moving back in with Fern was the latest in a series of mistakes. Nevertheless, I stayed with her for another year. We soon returned to what we were prior to my brief stint in Asheville: roommates masquerading as a couple. I slept next to her most nights but spent a good few evenings on the couch. On those nights I would stretch out on my back, my feet dangling off the edge of the couch, the room dark save for the car-lights passing every few minutes outside the window. When they moved across the room, I spied my books arranged carefully on shelves. My books that traveled with me across a time zone, from apartment to apartment, from Chicago to Asheville and then back again. In those moments in the dark, unable to find comfort on the tiny couch, I smiled.

Commute Reading

"There's time you can carve out in a day," said my friend, R.

Question: To what was he referring?

Answer: Finding time to read.

R. said this during a chat on Facebook. The chat was mostly about how little we're reading because of, among other factors, Facebook.

Qs: Is it necessary to carve out time to read? Why?

As: Yes. Because reading is important. Because when we lean into post-literacy, we stop exercising an important muscle.

Q: What important muscle?

A: Well, I'm no scientist, but I'm sure there are parts of the brain—we can, why not, call them muscles—that are exercised when we read, because reading is an active pursuit versus the passive option of watching TV or films, as fun as they can be.

When I state this, I sound like a preachy asshole. Nonetheless, I try to practice what I preach. Each morning, I bring a book to help make the 45-minute commute to work bearable. By reading on the train, I'm able to get through a fair number of books. I try to bring portable texts (poetry, mid-sized essay collections, novels not written by a Russian in the 19th century) and I try to focus. I can't read while listening to music, and I hate earbuds, so I let the natural sounds of the Chicago Transit Authority serve as my soundtrack. Subsequently, the last story I tried to get through while riding the subway train, "A Hunger Artist" by Franz Kafka, was processed as follows:

In the last decades interest in hunger artists has declined

COUGH! considerably. Whereas in earlier days *None of your fuckin' business, bitch* there was good money to be earned putting on major productions of this sort under one's own *COUGH!* management, nowadays that is totally impossible. Those were different times. *Fucking police… bitches.* Back then the hunger *MOTHER! Just… I can't. I just can't with you today!* artist captured the attention of the entire city. From day to day while the fasting lasted, participation *COUGH!* increased. Everyone wanted to see the hunger artist at least daily. During the final days there were people with subscription tickets who sat *I've been here all night / I've been here all day / And boy, got me walkin' side to side / Let them hoes know* all day in front of the small barred cage. And there were even *ATTENTION: THIS TRAIN WILL RUN EXPRESS FROM FULLERTON TO LAKE. REPEAT: WE WILL RUN EXPRESS FROM FULLERTON TO LAKE* viewing hours *Fuck!* at night, their *What'd she say?* impact heightened *Express to where?* by *COUGH!* torchlight.

I understand why Kafka is continually cited as a deeply strange and challenging writer.

Saturday with Kinzie and John Donne's Innuendos

2007, Evanston, IL

First impression of Professor Kinzie: prim and humorless, very much the image one might have of a veteran university professor. I'd heard talk of her, mostly warnings not to take her class or, if I did, not to take any other that term, as she liked to pile on reading and writing assignments. She was fond of formal poetry and insisted that her students memorize works by Robert Frost and John Donne. Impatient to get my degree, I took her workshop, the only class offered that term that would move me closer to the finish line. To be honest, I was excited to take the challenge. I wanted to push myself.

Day one was rough. Kinzie asked the room to discuss their favorite poets as a means of breaking the ice, and, I suspect, to judge us on our choices. When it was my turn, I mentioned Cesar Vallejo, whose *Trilce* I had been reading and enjoying.

"That's poetry in translation," she said. "Who do you like who writes in English?"

I couldn't think of a response. I was very into translated literature at that time and her dismissal of Vallejo annoyed me. Of course, now I see her point: she was going to attempt to teach me about the choices English writers make when they compose poems because we were writing in English. Translation theory is fascinating and certainly worthwhile, but it was not her concern in that class. I took her words as another in the long series of slights translated literature has received from the academy. My defenses went up. Unconsciously, I started to resist Kinzie's instruction.

The textbook, *A Poet's Guide to Poetry* by none other than Mary Kinzie, was another source of irritation. She actually made us buy her book and use it for the class. What goddamn gall! Using her class as a means of selling more books—this was an exercise of power, a self-serving action that made me furious. At the time it didn't occur to me that Kinzie was proud of her book, had put a lot of work into it, and that she might consider it the ideal text for teaching us, the spoiled philistines, about spondees, we who prostrated ourselves before the altar of free verse.

The text itself? Actually, a very good book on poetry, including insightful bits about how to approach the composition of poems, forms, rhetorical choices, diction, tension in lines, all that sort of thing. The argument she makes about the constraints of formal poetry being a necessary source of creativity is one that I'm now sympathetic to, even if I fought against it at the time. I was foolish and couldn't stand the idea of my poems being forced to fit into a scheme. I, like too many writers, thought free verse was liberating, even politically progressive. What utter horseshit.

Kinzie's voice has stayed with me over the years as well. She had an intimidating, direct manner of instruction that made us all a bit fearful. When she told me that I should consider whether my idea for a poem was sonnet worthy, I reacted with predictable rebellion, thinking: *Is the sonnet worthy of my idea!* How goddamn callow.

She gave me a B, a merciful grade. Actually, she didn't give me anything—I earned that B. But I saw that grade as something she placed upon me, not something I deserved. Truth be told: I was only working as hard as I needed to. What the hell did I expect?

Now that I'm the one tasked with evaluating students and assigning their efforts a symbol, grades seem so stupid to me. That's because I have my degree and my job, and I don't really remember what grades meant to me when I was a student. I forget the sting of that B. An A is the most important thing to some of my students. It is the thing that validates them. To others, an A is the grade they must earn if they're to maintain their scholarships or their standing as a part of an athletic team. I've gotten quite a few "If I don't get an A I'm going to get kicked off the golf team!" emails, to which I usually reply: "Our university has a golf team?"

To some students, a B is a fine grade, something they're happy to receive. I was not one of them, and so the B in Kinzie's class irked me. My otherwise perfect record (not counting the incredible amount of fucking off I did during my earlier time in higher education) was now blemished. And why? Because I wasn't very good at memorizing poems? Because I couldn't remember the pattern of dactylic hexameter? No. I got the B because I only put forth enough effort to earn the B.

I tried to explain that concept to a student who questioned his grade, a D. Why had I given him such a low mark? I went through the standard bit— "You earned the D all on your own"—but nothing I said stuck. He still saw the grade as a vindictive mark, a sign of my contempt for him. I likely felt the same about Kinzie.

I'm tempted to make my students memorize a poem. While appearing pointless, it can work a part of the brain that might otherwise be sluggish. Memorization is useful, and poems—especially the ones with fixed meter and rhymes—are built to be memorized. Kinzie asked us to do this twice. The first time I chose "Stopping by Woods on a Snowy Evening" by Robert Frost, as did the rest of my classmates. We didn't plan to memorize and recite the same poem, but Kinzie understood our motivation: "I see. The last line is repeated, so you only had to memorize fifteen lines instead of sixteen." She clucked her tongue and moved on, unimpressed with our efforts.

For the next go around, she assigned a specific poem for each of us to commit to memory. I was given "Holy Sonnet 14" by John Donne.

The night before I was scheduled to meet Kinzie and recite Donne, I was at a bar with some friends. I'd been reading and rereading the sonnet all day. I mentioned this to one of my friends, who asked me to recite the poem for him. I managed the first four lines.

"'Batter my heart, three-person'd God, for you
As yet but knock, breathe, shine, and seek to mend;
That I may rise and stand, o'erthrow me, and bend
Your force to break, blow, burn, and make me new.'"

"Dude, that sounds dirty."
"What?"
"Bend me over. Break me. Blow."
"C'mon."
"Seriously, that sounds like fucking. Who wrote this?"
"John Donne."
"He must've had sex on the mind."
"I don't think so."
"I know what I heard."
"This is a Holy Sonnet. That's what it's called."
"Whose hole are we talking about?"
"Oh Jesus…"

Of course, I fucked up the recitation the next day. Kinzie had me meet her at a café in Evanston, and I got there early enough to down a few espressos before she arrived, which only made me more nervous than I was already. My memory of the poem was imperfect, and my instructor was intimidating. I felt like a fraud. What the hell was I doing studying poetry? I should go back to the warehouses and blue-collar jobs that spawned me. I didn't belong in the ivory tower.

Kinzie was generous. She smiled when I flubbed the final couplet, congratulated me on my efforts, and spoke to me like I was a human being.

"You're definitely passionate," she said. "That's good. But you should focus your passion a bit."

"Okay," I said, unsure of what that meant.

"Your last round during the workshop showed some progress."

I may have blushed.

Years later, I realize how unfair I was to Kinzie, how my

resistance to her teaching was foolish. I'm humbled by her erudition, commitment, and frankness. She wasn't Tom Sullivan. She wasn't there to be my friend, but that Saturday when we met at the café, she made me aware that while my attitude and posturing would only take me so far, I was nevertheless in possession of the passion necessary to keep going. I need only learn some focus and discipline. I'm still working on that.

Correspondence

November 3, 2016

Dear BestSellers,

I'm writing today to comment on the quality of *After the Tall Timber: Collected Nonfiction* by Renata Alder. You described the condition of the book as "Used—Very Good" and stated that the cover showed "Minimal wear." This prompted me to purchase the book, though, upon inspecting the item, which was delivered today, I was shocked to find a large stain on the cover, surely the result of a cup of coffee. Forgetting for a moment that there are monsters in the world who use hardback books as coasters, I would've expected you to either, 1. clean the stain by using some sort of damp cloth, or, 2. mention the stain in your description. Also, the significant tear to the dust jacket is concerning. Shouldn't you have included that in the description as well?

I realize the item was sold to me for only $4.95, a fraction of the cover price, but I nevertheless expect a certain standard when buying books online. I'm not seeking redress, but I thought you should know what prompted my 2-star rating.

Yours,

Vincent Francone

November 4, 2016

Dear Mr. Francone,

Thank you for reaching out to us with your concern. We apologize if the item was not what you expected. Though we do our best to ensure that our items are in good shape and securely packed, sometimes things can happen during the shipping process. If you'd like a refund, let us know and we'll send details on how to facilitate that transaction.

Sincerely,
BestSellers

November 4, 2016
Dear BestSellers,

Thanks for the quick reply, but I wonder if you sent me a stock email. Obviously, the book did not get stained while tightly packed in a box and shipped across the country unless a postal clerk removed the item, bought coffee, placed their leaking cup on the book, and repacked it. You may also note that I stated I don't want my money back, but that I was pointing out why I only gave you a 2-star rating, so no, I don't need information on how to obtain a refund. I do want the book—I just wish it was in better shape, or that you had adequately described it before I bought it. Of course, if you're offering to refund my money without me having to return the book, I'd not say no.

Vincent Francone

November 7, 2016
Dear Mr. Francone,

I apologize. Our last message was an automatic reply that is sent when someone makes a complaint. I see from your first email that you don't want a refund and were just trying to let us know where we fell short. I want to apologize for that as well.

I appreciate that you don't want your money back, but I'm going to process a refund anyway as a means of fully expressing my regret.

Thank you,
Eric Sellers
President of BestSellers

November 8, 2016

Dear Mr. Sellers,

Thanks for the refund, but I feel like a jerk—I was just trying to explain why I rated you so low, not get my money back. $4.95 is not a lot to ask for a hardback book like this one, and I should know that "you get what you pay for" and not to expect a pristine book for such a low price.

Cancel the refund.

V. Francone

November 8, 2016

Mr. Francone,

The refund request has already been processed. It should post to your bank account in a few days. It's a bit late to reverse it, and, frankly, doing so would be a pain. Will you just take the money?

Eric Sellers

November 9, 2016

Mr. Sellers,

Ugh. I'm so sorry. I never should've mentioned the refund. Maybe I never should've written to you at all. I've really opened a can of worms (forgive the cliché) and I regret all of this. Tell you what— I'll buy something else from your store. It's the least I can do.

Best,

V.

November 10, 2016

Mr. Francone,

Do what you like. Buy something. From us or from anyone. Either way, you're getting that $4.95 back.

November 10, 2016

Mr. Sellers,

I hate to ask, but will the refund include the shipping cost?
Just wondering.
V.

November 11, 2016
Mr. Francone,
No. I'm afraid the cost of shipping and handling is non-refundable. The book was sent. It cost us money to send it. The best we can do is refund the $4.95 since the book is damaged, but the shipping and handling are a different matter entirely.
Eric Sellers

November 12, 2016
Mr. Sellers,
I understand that shipping costs exist in a different place (perhaps a different dimension) than the cost of an item, and that shipping prices are not set by you but are dictated by the post office. However, I'm unsure what "handling" is and why it's something I need to pay for. If handling means, as I suspect, the act of packing a book, I might suggest that the seller cover such fees. Or would you charge a customer in a store every time they forced you to ring them up at the cash register?
Anyway, I never wanted a refund in the first place, so no need to get indignant when I ask a simple follow-up question.
V.

November 13, 2016
Mr. Francone,
Do you have any understanding of commerce? Handling is a cost assumed by the customer, not the seller. Your analogy is ridiculous. We wouldn't charge people for making us use the register, but when we set our prices, we do consider the expense of the plastic bags we place sold items in. Things like plastic bags and shipping materials cost us money. In order to stay profitable, we have to figure

in those costs when we charge for services. That's how this works. Maybe you'd prefer that we gave you everything for free? Well that's not going to happen.

Do me a favor and take the $4.95 refund and never buy anything else from us again. And by the way, in case you are unaware, a portion of the money we make through our Amazon store goes to a local charity. Sorry if your book wasn't in 100% perfect shape, but the lousy $4.95 you spent for the thing was supposed to help a local shelter. So, I hope you're happy. Some kid is now going hungry because you're pissed about a goddamn coffee stain on a perfectly readable book.

I hope you sleep well in your comfortable bed surrounded by your precious books, asshole.

Eric Sellers

December 3, 2016

Dear Mr. Sellers,

Sorry to bother you again. After the last message I figured it best to leave things alone, but I see you're selling a copy of *The Poems of Velimir Khlebnikov* described as "Used—Very Good" and, as there is no other used copy on Amazon under $45.00, I wanted to purchase the copy you have for sale. But I wanted to make sure the "Used—Very Good" is accurate. Can you offer a more detailed description of the book? Any tears to the dust jacket? Foxing? Stains? Writing or highlighting? How's the binding? Tight? The spine in good shape?

Thanks in advance,

Vince Francone

December 4, 2016

Go fuck yourself.

Eric Sellers

Q.

I was resistant to getting a new dog because I'm still grieving. I said as much to a neighbor who recommended that I adopt a dog from the local shelter.

"It's too soon," I said.

His response: "There're a lot of dogs who need a loving home and don't have the time to wait for people to get through their grief."

This is how we came to adopt a new dog, Q., short for Queequeg, the most loyal and savage character from *Moby-Dick*.

This new dog is ugly and cute in that way only dogs and Willem Dafoe can pull off. My wife thinks he looks like Klaus Kinski. The little pooch certainly has the same intense look, especially when he sees another dog trespassing on his territory. This territory is comprised of the entire block on which we live. Any dog in sight is an intruder.

We assume Q., in the time before he came to live with us, was confined to a backyard and never walked on a leash. He had no idea what to do when we fitted him with a harness and attached the long strip of leather. He pulls on his leash and refuses to walk in a set pattern, following the dictates of his nose. If we cross another dog, a growl emerges from our little guy, followed by a quick bark, then a series of sounds I never knew could come from anything of this world.

His breath is repugnant and seems to gain in strength immediately after I brush his teeth. One lower fang refuses to stay in his mouth, creating a permanent snarl. His breeding is uncertain, but it's likely Chihuahua mixed with opossum. He's a blond shaggy creature with brown eyes and a bit of white on the muzzle evincing age if not maturity. His hobbies include sitting on my hands as I type, sneezing in my mouth, and howling when he hears bagpipes. Cassandra finds this funny, thus there's a lot of bagpipe music played in my apartment, ensuring canine accompaniment.

The things I do for this dog.

He cannot be left alone for more than a few hours. If I chance a long night out, I'll return to find the couches pissed on. He sometimes has a queasy belly and will eat stray hairs and dust bunnies to make himself vomit. The vomit has the consistency of a feline hairball, making me suspect he is part cat, though he doesn't have the same level of aloof intelligence.

When we first got him, I wasn't sure how to bond with the guy. Not ready to let myself be emotionally vulnerable, I must've unconsciously distanced myself from this blond monster encroaching on my personal space. But soon I started to enjoy waking to the sight of his unkempt ears and the weight of his ten pounds on my chest.

The dog loves me. He follows me from room to room. He waits for me outside the bathroom until I'm finished. He looks at me with eyes that suggest he could never be anything other than innocent. It helps assuage the hostility he inspires during our walks when he refuses to listen.

"Don't sniff that. Don't you dare pee there. Wait for me. Don't pull. Stay. *Stay*. STAY!"

I thought I might try to read to Q. the way I used read to my other dog who was content to listen to poems by Seamus Heaney or a novel by Georgi Gospodinov. But this is not my other dog. This is my now dog. My oddball dog who wants to be with me all the time. My dog whose breath stinks, who howls in his sleep and is currently sticking his nose in my lap as I type on a laptop computer. This is my dog for today. And any day with a dog is a good day.

He's won me over.

Last night I found myself sticking my face in his side as he slept and kissing his fur. And I thought about my other dog. And I cried. Then I kissed Q. again. He licked my face and went back to sleep, enviably content.

I just read this to my dog. He was unimpressed, but he'll get excited when I stand up. We're going for a walk now. I'll likely feel less fond of this beast while we walk, but when we get in, after I clean mud off his paws, I'll kiss him between his pronounced ears and thank the little prick for being with me today.

Confession Time

Like a lot of people, I've lied about finishing books that I've abandoned. Rather than admit that I couldn't get through *The Idiot* or *The Grapes of Wrath,* I, when asked, say that yes, I have read these books. I've banked on the interlocutor ceasing their inquiry, and I've been lucky inasmuch as they probably haven't read *The Idiot* or *The Grapes of Wrath* either. I'm sure we were both simultaneously worried that one of us would ask a question or mention a detail that would unmask the other. But the fear of exposure kept us from making a sloppy mistake. We're not going to lie about books we haven't done some cursory research into. I can discuss *Madame Bovary* without having finished it. I know enough about *Middlemarch* to chime in a bit without really giving away that I've not made it past page 50. My discussion of these or any of the many books I've perused without finishing is well informed. Nevertheless, I'm fearful that, at the cocktail party of the future, I will, after one drink too many, utter some giveaway that will reveal me for the fraud I am.

Most nights I prefer to watch TV. The days are long. I teach my classes, grade my papers, attend my meetings, then—if there's energy left—write a bit. When it's time to end my workday, I'm happiest with a drink on the couch, a dog on my lap, and the seemingly endless distractions of cable TV and Netflix. I bring a book with me to the couch, tell myself that I'll just see if anything good is on, scroll through the channels, settle on a cooking competition, tell myself that I'll watch it to the end, just to see who wins the dessert round, see the book waiting to be read, feel guilty for not reading it, tell myself that I'll just catch the end of a movie on cable that I've seen five times already, finish the movie, see the book again, feel more guilt, flip through a few pages, decide my eyes need a rest, watch a *Seinfeld* rerun, close my eyes and listen to the sound of familiar sitcom dialogue. An hour later, I wake to the sound of another *Seinfeld* rerun and the book at my side or, sometimes, under the dog who's using it as a sort of pillow. I then decide that it's time to read, though I see the clock and realize that I'm supposed to meet Cassandra after she gets off work. I bring the book with me in case there's a lull in our evening, though, more times than not, the book goes unread. We return to the apartment. I place the book back on the shelf where it will go unread for another day. *I'll read it tomorrow*, I think. *There's always tomorrow.*

I'm likely not alone. Many of us don't read as much as we feel we should. Thankfully, there are ways to mask our functional illiteracy. The next time you're at a cocktail party and someone asks you about a book you haven't read, choose one of the following replies:

- Please, don't get me started on [name of author]. [His/her] prose is turgid and lifeless. I'd sooner read a grocery list.
- I found it to be didactic without being preachy.
- Oh yes, I gave it a whirl. Didn't hate it. Some real tension in the story, but I read it so long ago I've forgotten most of the details.
- Ambitious to a fault, but not without its charms.
- The book showed promise. I'm more interested in what [he/she] will write next.
- Good, but it could've used some editing. The last chunk was a bit slow.
- I think I need to reread it to get a better sense of what the writer was trying to say.
- I wouldn't sully myself with such trash.

Any of the above comments will put your party companion on edge and end the conversation. If you're lucky, they'll never again bother you about the books you haven't read. Maybe they'll stop asking you to cocktail parties and you can stay home and watch Netflix. Bye bye Thomas Pynchon, hello *Jessica Jones*.

Stupid Men

"What's *A Moveable Feast?*"

"The Hemingway book?"

"Yeah, I see it on the shelf. Actually… two copies."

"Yeah, a hardback and a paperback."

"You need two copies?"

"It's a good book. Really, the only one by Hemingway I'd go back to. I tried to reread *A Farewell to Arms* a while ago and didn't get far."

"It's not good?"

"I liked it a lot when I read it, but it annoyed me when I tried to read it again. The dialogue is crap. And the woman in the book is poorly written. A perfect example of a man trying to write a woman and failing."

"It's hard for men to write women, I guess. And dialogue seems difficult."

"It is, but Hemingway doesn't even try. But it didn't bother me as much in *A Moveable Feast.*"

"Why not?"

"I don't know. *A Moveable Feast* is supposed to be a memoir, but it's so clearly bullshit. I like that—memoirs are full of lies, so there's something about Hemingway's that I admire. His bullshit is transparent. It's refreshing."

"So, bullshit dialogue is okay as long as it's in a memoir?"

"I guess. It's hard to explain. Novels try so hard to create a realistic world. Even fantasy and sci-fi—they lay on so much detail to try to get the reader to believe. Memoirs have an advantage: they present themselves as truth and people just go along with it, so really, they get to bend the truth and invent as much as a piece of imagination, but they're sort of liberated from having to establish details that would convince a reader. They just proclaim THIS IS A TRUE STORY and that's enough."

"No, not really. Readers can see through obvious bullshit, right?"

"Nah. Look at that James Frey guy. He suckered millions of people when a critical reading of chapter one should've been enough to clue people in. The book was so obviously full of exaggeration and fiction, but readers were willing to believe. I think they're more careful and judgmental when they approach fiction. You really can't let any seams show or people will pounce. They're looking for flaws because they know going in that they're reading a lie."

"So, you don't believe Hemingway's book?"

"No, but I don't care. It's about Paris in the '20s. Joyce and Fitzgerald and Ezra Pound and Gertrude Stein are in it. It's great stuff. And Hemingway has to give Scott Fitzgerald a pep talk about the size of his cock."

"Hemingway's or Fitzgerald's?"

"Fitzgerald's. Zelda told him he had a small penis and it really got to him, so Hemingway has him whip out his dick for assessment. Then Hemingway takes Fitzgerald to see some nude sculptures to put it into perspective."

"Oh my god. Who cares?"

"What do you mean?"

"This is what these two so-called giants of American literature did? They talked about their dicks?"

"Well... allegedly. But it's funny, right?"

"You men are so ridiculous. That insult really gets to you, doesn't it?"

"I suppose so."

"You're so vulnerable about that. So scared that you don't have what it takes. How stupid."

"But you believe that, don't you?"

"What?"

"That two men would talk about that. That a woman could hurt a man that easily, by suggesting he has a small dick. That rings true, right?"

"Yes, unfortunately."

"I mean, it's too dumb to be made up."

"Sounds like Hemingway was shit at writing women, but he knew men very well."

Bios

My first bio was as silly as any out there. Let's get that stated immediately.

I know the thrill of being published, however small the journal, and as if that ego stroke were not enough, the request for a short author bio can turn the humblest of us insufferable.

Cuteness is a sort of reaction against pomposity. I get that, but in thumbing our noses in the faces of the tweed and leather elbow patch gang, we've essentially created a cadre of clever lit pricks that make the ultra-serious seem less pretentious by comparison.

My first bio makes me cringe. I mentioned that I prefer poblano peppers to jalapenos. Why? Because my lack of publishing credits embarrassed me. Because I was sure I didn't belong to the Writers Club, so I tried to hide behind this unimportant item. I'd seen plenty of bios with cute factoids like mine, so I aped other green writers. It's a useless quirk, certainly not worth sharing, but there it is, still up on the website of a small press that's somehow endured for over a decade.

A friend has finished editing an edition of a reputable literary journal. Half the published writers are what one calls "established" and the others are "emerging." The emerging have cute bios. They read like this:

Summer Wilson is an adjective doing her best to be who she thinks she is. Check out her Instagram.

Born of a chance encounter while a million sperm were vying to reach one lonely egg, Kimberly Dang has called three continents home and is searching for her true muse.

radley valiant writes things, makes films, and talks to anyone who'll listen. His work in progress is a 1,000+ page MS detailing the inner thoughts of the first dog launched into space called The Horrible Beauty.

If you see Grant Mueller on the street, say hello and buy him tacos.

Molly Ketchum is a poet, blogger, flash fictionist, bicycle enthusiast, rock collector, radical vegan, multi-modal conceptualist, thinker, and drum circle sista from Portland, Oregon. Holla at her Twitter feed.

If these bios smack of youthful exuberance, well, nothing wrong with that. And if they clash with the seasoned, serious, more accomplished writers, that's fine too. Neither youthful nor seasoned, I've decided to update my bio and rid it of winking cuteness and ostentation. Only the essentials, damnit. Here goes:

Vincent Francone is a writer from Chicago whose work has appeared in Spectrum, Rhino, New City, The Oklahoma Review, and other web and print journals. He won 1ˢᵗ place in the 2009 Illinois Emerging Writers Competition and his memoir, Like a Dog, *was published in the fall of 2015 by Blue Heron Book Works, LLC. Visit his website www.vincentfrancone.com to learn more and see pictures of his dog.*

Not too shaggy, though the first thing to go is the mention of my dog. Sure, I have a lot of pictures of him on my website, but no one needs to know that. Anyway, if they click on the site, they'll see those pictures. And does anyone need to know which journals I've been published in? The only reason to share specific titles is to impress, and none of the ones I've listed are going to make people go "Oh, wow!" so, yep, they're gone. And what does it matter where I'm from? Chicago… cut! And I'm a writer? How fucking pompous. And that bit about my publisher? Info like that is easily found, so, yeah, let's get rid of it.

The revised bio:

> *Vincent Francone's work has appeared in many web and print journals. He won 1ˢᵗ place in the 2009 Illinois Emerging Writers Competition and his memoir,* Like a Dog, *was published in the fall of 2015. Visit his website www.vincentfrancone.com to learn more.*

From 68 to 42 words. Nice. But really, I think I might chop it down a bit further. If I'm relying on only the important stuff, the bio might simply read:

> *Vincent Francone's work has appeared in many journals. He won 1ˢᵗ place in the Illinois Emerging Writers Competition and his memoir,* Like a Dog, *was published in the fall of 2015. Visit his website www.vincentfrancone.com.*

Better still. I lost the "web and print" distinction and cut the "to learn more" part, as it doesn't seem necessary. Ditto the "2009" as it doesn't matter when I won that award. Well, truth be told, I cut that bit because it seems so long ago, and the obvious follow up question is: what the hell have you been up to since then? The answer is the memoir but to state that it was published in 2015, six years after winning a literary award, implies that I'm slow writer, one who isn't churning out the proper amount of publishable pages. Come to think of it, the "2015" part can go. So now we have:

> *Vincent Francone's work has appeared in journals. He won 1ˢᵗ place in the Illinois Emerging Writers Competition. His memoir is titled* Like a Dog. *www.vincentfrancone.com.*

Down to 25 words!

Brevity being the soul of wit, I figure the shorter the better. This is why I simply end with the web address and lose the whole "visit his website" lead-in. People know what the hell to do with a web link. And the web link takes them to my site, which has all the biographical info they could ever need. That stated, why am I even bothering to mention the 1st place win of that literary contest? And why bother mentioning the memoir? Maybe the bio should simply read:

Vincent Francone. www.vincentfrancone.com.

Now I've got it! Lean and mean. Just my name and the web address. But might I not simply list the link and call it a day?

www.vincentfrancone.com.

Truly this is the least pretentious, least cloyingly cute bio ever written.

I showed my cut-to-the-bone bio to my friend the editor. He was not impressed.

"Too stripped."

"Maybe, but at least I lost all the self-congratulatory stuff. Who wants to read that anyway?"

"But you shouldn't shy away from adding some fun to the bio."

"I hate cute bios."

"That's because you have no joy. So naturally you react with hostility when you see other people expressing their joy."

I want to believe that this is not the case, but the guy might have a point. Maybe I was too harsh in my condemnation of the youthfully cheerful bio. With that in mind, I've redrafted my bio to reflect my inner *joie de vivre*:

Vincent Francone will cook you the best dish of huevos con tortilla you've ever tasted. His golf game is nonexistent, but he's a mean skeeballer. He prefers poblano peppers to jalapenos. Go to www.vincentfrancone.com and challenge him to a Monty Python trivia duel.

"Jesus, what are you, 22 years old?" said my editor friend.

"I was trying to be clever and fun."

"You sound like a child."

"Well, what should I write?"

"How about being honest and revealing. That's what people want to see. Don't hold back, don't be coy, and don't be so silly."

With that in mind, I refined the bio. I think it's the best version yet:

Vincent Francone likes poached eggs but is too lazy, or maybe too scared, to try poaching them at home. Subsequently, he consumes far too many fried eggs, which are worse for the body. This is but one example of how his life is altered negatively due to his inability to confront fears. He lives in Rogers Park, a part of Chicago that he describes thusly: "Hippies, college students, gang bangers, trees." He drinks a nightly nightcap that grows in size as his memory simultaneously shrinks. He spends his days teaching bored freshman how to avoid comma splice errors and imagines that he'll retire via a weighing stone tossed into Lake Michigan. He prefers poblano peppers to jalapenos, though both—like damn near anything he puts into his body—are likely to cause indigestion. His intake of snacks is at pace with his eating of antacids. He somehow convinced a woman to marry him. He has a history of being a lousy boyfriend. He once told a nun to go fuck herself. He's a lapsed catholic, but the incident still haunts his conscience. A member of the Christian Brothers once called him a cynical bastard. The author is at work on a strange book about his love of books. The text is currently spinning out of control and getting more absurd by the minute. What started as a somewhat somber meditation on his deceased dog has become considerably less marketable. His publisher is beside herself. Visit his website www.vincentfrancone.com to send him an angry message that he'll take to heart. Go on, you know you want to hurt the fucker.

How Not to Propose Marriage

2010, Tunisia

When travelling through Tunisia, one should not carry an engagement ring. At least not for very long. And if one is in the position of having an engagement ring with them, and if they are looking to keep that ring a secret, then perhaps a better place to store the ring could be found than the inside of a slim book of poems.

I know a thing or two about this. I visited Tunisia a year before the Arab Spring revolution that would spread most famously to Egypt. I was not witness to the country's upheaval, though there were tense moments during the trip, most notably the last morning in this beautiful country at the top of Africa.

I was travelling with Cassandra. She's Cassandra for a reason, specifically her ability to know the future and her frustration at my reluctance to heed her predictions. My failure to take her soothsayerism seriously might make me a tragic figure akin to Agamemnon, but I lack that grandeur. I'm just thickheaded.

The night before we were scheduled to fly back to Chicago from Tunis, Cassandra was worried that her friend, Ali, who agreed to take us to the airport, would oversleep. Our flight was early, and she suggested we start making backup arrangements. She was all too aware of Ali's casual relationship with time.

"It'll be fine. He promised to pick us up. Anyway, we'll call a cab if he's late."

My assurances were hesitantly accepted. We packed our bags and went to bed early.

It was—I dunno—5:00 AM? We were woken by the call to

prayer, an agonized supplication to God blasted through faulty speakers. The Tunisian sun had yet to rise. Bleary-eyed, stomach afire, I managed to get ready for the ride to the airport.

An hour after the call to prayer, Ali was nowhere to be found. No answer on his phone.

"Maybe we'd better call a cab?" I offered.

"Maybe," Cassandra said, raising an eyebrow and tightening her lips.

"We'll be fine," I said.

I couldn't find a taxi company. Nothing came of my search on my primitive cellular phone and nothing resembling a Yellow Pages directory was in sight. I dialed 411, but the call went nowhere. This was another continent, after all; foolish of me to assume my American conveniences would extend across an ocean.

Cassandra usually doesn't have trouble saying, "I told you so," but the thought of missing our flight kept her quiet. She gathered our bags while I scrambled to find alternative means of transportation. I was soon reduced to cursing in order to fill the growing void in the room.

"Where the fuck is he?"

"I don't know."

"What'll we do?"

Cassandra shot me a look that told me not to ask questions in the AM that should've been addressed the previous PM.

Ali showed at the last possible minute. Groggy, still in last night's clothes, he apologized. We didn't bother to listen to his excuses, just threw our bags in his car and buckled up.

Ali sped to get us to the airport in time for our flight. And, saints be praised, he made it there with a little time to spare. But when he zipped through the airport and screeched to a halt in the passenger drop-off lane, two police officers took notice. They flagged him down and began their interrogation. My instinct was to offer Ali a hasty goodbye and begin checking in, but the officers told him that we were not permitted to enter the airport. Possessing no Arabic skills, Cassandra and I were powerless to protest.

Ali did his best to reason with the police, or so it seemed. Honestly, I have no idea what he said to them, but he seemed to be pleading with the uniformed men with big guns. Not knowing what else to do, Cassandra and I kept silent. I was quite sure that behind her silence she had a lot to say. I might hear some of it if we ever got into the airport and out of the country.

Ali slipped the officers some money and we were on our way. It was as simple as that. Had I known that some dinar would get us into the airport, I would've gladly offered all I had.

Cassandra held back. She could've restated last night's predication about Ali's inherent tardiness, dwelling on my dismissal of her concerns.

"I'm Cassandra, remember," she might've said.

"Exactly—which means you have to expect that no one will heed your warnings."

"Bullshit. You've read enough Greek tragedy to know how this goes. The reader is permitted dramatic irony and can see what'll happen."

"Ah, but dramatic irony doesn't allow the characters to know what's coming, only the viewers of the play."

"Hey, you're the lit major. You ought to know better. Don't be some tragic figure. Listen to Cassandra when she talks."

But she didn't say a word along those lines, just asked me if I wanted coffee now that we were in the airport and safely through security.

"A coffee would be great."

As I brought the cup to my lips, she said, "You're going to burn yourself."

I froze, heeding her warning at last. She's Cassandra. She knows the future.

Despite the stressful exit, our vacation was pleasurable. I'd never before thought of venturing to Tunisia. I'd never met anyone who'd put that country high on their list of places to visit. So why was I in

North Africa?

Here's why:

While enrolled as an undergrad, Cassandra spent a few weeks studying in Tunisia. During this study abroad, she made friends, one of them, Ali, a lovely young man who told her he was to be married soon and invited her to return for the wedding.

"Don't you want to go to a Tunisian wedding?" Cassandra asked.

"It's always been a dream of mine. Hell, of every young boy!"

Sarcasm aside, I wasn't opposed, though I didn't think we'd go. Dreams of adventures through North Africa—like dreams of Europe or South America or other spots on the globe—have a habit of remaining dreams, things we discuss when imagining a time in the future when money and leisure are ample.

Cassandra knew I was being a smartass, but she told Ali that we were coming. He made considerable plans for our arrival, securing us accommodations and vouchers that would get us into tourist sites and museums. Cassandra informed me of his arrangements, and when I demonstrated some surprise— "You were *serious?*"—she told me what I already knew: there was no way we were not going after so much fuss had been made on our behalf.

It's unfair to make blanket statements (even when they're complimentary) based on a small dataset, but here goes: Tunisians are incredibly friendly and close to masochistic when it comes to making guests feel welcome. During the course of our time in Tunis, our host, Ali, procured a room for us in a home occupied by some family members. Mohammed and Noor, our incredibly generous hosts, sacrificed their master bedroom and a good deal of their personal comfort for us. They didn't say a word when we started each day with a shower, though I now suspect our cavalier use of their water—probably an expensive luxury—was presumptuous. Such ugly Americans.

One evening, Noor hurt her ankle. We insisted she sleep in her own bed that night, but her response was an emphatic "No." We couldn't persuade her to leave the couch. I appealed to her son, Ayman, with whom I'd been spending considerable time playing poker and discussing *The Simpsons* and Metallica.

"You mother is being generous to a fault."

"She's made up her mind," he said. "There's no changing her mind when she's made it up."

We resumed playing cards and watching reruns of *Boston Legal*, a popular show in Tunis at the time. Ayman knew more about American television than I did.

"Are American streets like Wisteria Lane?" he asked.

"What's that?"

"You know, from *Desperate Housewives*."

"Oh, yeah. Some of them," I said, not having the heart to tell him that I didn't watch the show.

Ayman was always with us. He decided that it was his duty to escort us through the streets of Tunis and beyond, accompanying us on a train ride to see the Roman amphitheater in El Djem as well as The Bardo National Museum and all throughout the labyrinthine Tunis Medina. At no time during these outings was I able to propose marriage to Cassandra, which I was dead set on doing while in Tunisia. She loved the country. It boasts breathtakingly gorgeous landscapes and certainly would be a better place to ask her the big question than Chicago—too many people have used up the landmarks of our city. We both love the Chagall mosaic *Four Seasons* on Dearborn, but it's a site where many a question has been popped. No way was I going to drag Cassandra there to propose marriage.

When not in the company of our guide Ayman, we were surrounded by cousins and uncles and an extended family whose members I couldn't keep straight. The core of the family, the ones we sat and sipped tea with each evening, were beyond accommodating, but even the people who showed up to only one event—who, despite being introduced, I was not likely to remember—were excessively hospitable. Subsequently, I often forgot who to thank. The week was one big, lovable Tunisian blur of faces.

Days were spent seeing sights—a fun albeit exhausting pursuit—but each evening there was a party or a ritual that required observance. The night we arrived, a cow was slaughtered. The father of the bride, Sami, had purchased the cow, which Cassandra named Azraq. A beautiful animal, Azraq was felled with a rope and some sharp knives as we watched in horror. Only a few short hours prior, Cassandra had pet the animal and granted her the dignity of a proper name. Now she was uncooked meat and bone. We tried to explain to our hosts and new friends that we didn't eat meat, though we, of course, reserved no judgment for those who do. Try explaining vegetarianism to people who don't have the luxury of buying hamburgers and fried chicken every minute of the day. Watch for the confused look on their faces.

After we'd had enough grisly slaughter, we went into the kitchen where the women were singing and dancing while water boiled and bread baked. There was no booze, but I managed to drink my body weight in coffee while doing my best to move to the spontaneous music without looking more foolish than I usually do. And I succeeded, sort of—dancing among my new Tunisian friends came naturally. None of them were executing practiced moves so much as moving to the percussion and having a good time. I've never felt more relaxed when trying to dance. These stiff bones actually neared something close to graceful movement.

Another day, another botched chance to propose: Cassandra and I went to see Carthage outside the city, with Ayman, of course. I asked the kid if he might get scarce for a while, leaving me alone with my girlfriend and, hopefully, soon-to-be fiancée.

"But you should not be alone!"

"Why?"

"It's not safe."

"Do you mean this is a dangerous area?"

"No," he said. "It's not that."

"So, what could happen?"

"You could get lost! You could get used!"

Getting *used* was what Ayman called getting ripped off. It was true, there were a few Tunisians who'd tried to swindle us Westerners. Were it not for Ayman, a cab driver would've liberated us from a more sizable amount of our money than we owed. Nevertheless, Ayman's fear that everyone was out to steal from us seemed far-fetched. And, as a seasoned traveler, I've reconciled myself to being cheated a bit. Cassandra and I were once stranded in a bus station in a godforsaken part of Villahermosa, Mexico. We had to wait eight hours for the next bus, time we spent playing cards. At one point, Cassandra sent me to a small shop for some water and snacks. In my busted-up Spanish, I asked for the total amount of pesos I had to sacrifice for a bottle of water and a bag of nasty looking cookies. The clerk told me, and, in my weary state of mind, I gave him a bigger bill than I should have. He gave me a lot less change than I was owed. Back at the bus station, I realized my error, but there was no way I was going to insist he refund me the money. It happens.

Ayman wouldn't budge. I resigned myself to carrying the ring for another day. Every few minutes I'd rub my fingers over the space where it was nestled not very safely in my pocket. *Tomorrow*, I told myself. *I'll figure out a way to ask her tomorrow.*

Upon our return from the Roman ruins, the women informed me that Cassandra was theirs for the remainder of the evening. I found out later from Ayman and Ali that this was part of the week-long marital ceremony: the women visit an iconic spot to ask for a blessing of the union. They also visit one of the ancient bathhouses, sing songs and then get dressed in traditional garb and enjoy a large dinner that goes on until the small hours of the night. This dinner didn't break up until well past 1:00 AM. No men were allowed. While Cassandra was enjoying sororal bonding, I was left to listen to the men argue about soccer in Arabic for the better part of three hours before Ali, sensing my discomfort, whisked me away to a café. I was dying for a drink, but I knew better than to ask for alcohol. Tunisia is a mostly secular country, but my hosts were practicing Muslims. No need to be a fully ugly American.

While at the café, Ali and I talked about his impending nuptials. He seemed both exhilarated and exhausted by the process. The entire week he'd been helping his future in-laws, driving us to-and-from the house where we were staying to various attractions, and doing whatever he could to make everyone feel comfortable. I was feeling spent by mere sightseeing; I can't imagine how he felt.

"Are you thinking of getting married?" he asked.

I didn't want take attention away from him and his bride.

"I dunno. Maybe," I said.

"Maybe? You should think about this seriously. What else will you do with your life? What kind of life will you have without her?"

"Oh, I'm not romanticizing my bachelor freedom, if that's what you mean."

He might not have understood me. He didn't address my comment, only told me, "She's a very good woman. You should think about how lucky you are."

We drove back to Old Ariana in the north of Tunis where the women were still dining and laughing. We could hear them inside, all of us men standing in an alley waiting for the sisterly episode to conclude. Neither Ali nor Aymen smoked, but one of the cousins, Aziz, lit up. I asked him for a cigarette, my first in a while. This cigarette, a local brand called Mars, was rougher than the last Marlboro I'd smoked. Out of habit, I inhaled deeply, resulting in a serious coughing fit. The men laughed.

"It's been a while," I offered as an excuse.

"They hurt, I know," said Ali.

"I'm used to Marlboros or Camels."

"What about camels?"

"Never mind."

Cassandra emerged from the dinner dressed gorgeously, her head loosely covered in a hijab, her face rosy from a long night of laughing. I wanted very much to ask her then under those stars, *Will you marry me?* And I would've were we alone, though she may not have liked me getting down on one knee there in that filthy alley. I slid my hand in my jacket pocket, fingered the ring and told myself there was still time.

Cassandra decided that the one place we might visit on our own was Sidi Bou Saïd, a beautiful seaside town outside Tunis. She'd wanted to show me the shops, the cafés and the sea that looked toward Sicily. We arranged to be dropped off and readied ourselves for a day of walking through hilly streets and marveling at the blue and white buildings atop the Mediterranean. And it would just be the two of us.

As we planned to leave for Sidi Bou Saïd, Cassandra asked me why I was wearing a jacket. It was warm. No need for the extra layer. I'd stashed the ring in my coat pocket the day before, but Cassandra wasn't going to be seen with me if I wore a jacket in the heat.

"You look like one of the homeless guys that walk around wearing tons of layers all summer."

Not knowing what else to do, I sandwiched the ring between the pages of Medbh McGuckian's *The Book of the Angel*. A thin text of only 87 pages, it seemed more secure there than in the pockets of my worn-out khakis.

"Why'd you bring a book?" Cassandra asked. The question had no answer, at least none I could share. Outside of the fact that the book was conveyance for an engagement ring that, to be truthful, I was considering giving her immediately just to at last be free of the fucking thing, I never know what to say when she asks me this question. And it's a question I still get from her. We sit down to breakfast at some café or bistro and I hear, "Why'd you bring a book?" The implication seems to be that I find her company so tedious that I must bring a distraction, which is not the case. Cassandra knows me better than anyone. She ought to know that I always have a book on me, even if the occasion doesn't call for one. We go to movies; I bring a book. (You never know—I may have time before the trailers begin.) We go on road trips; I bring a book. (Road trips usually include stops at shops and stores I have no interest in, so why not have something to read?) We go for lunch; I bring a book. (The one time I didn't, Cassandra spent considerable time playing with her new smartphone, leaving me feeling ignored, angry, and wondering what the hell possessed me to leave my book at home.) But this was picturesque Sidi Bou Saïd—why on earth would I bring a book to this most beautiful of settings?

Why indeed. I couldn't tell her the truth, not yet. Instead, I shrugged my shoulders and said nothing, promptly irritating her.

We walked for a while. I was getting anxious. I had to get rid of the goddamn ring. I'd had it in my pocket for four days. It travelled across an ocean with me, then from city to city in North Africa. Now it was inside a thin paperback book of poems. Or was it? I checked on the ring when I could, desperate to ensure it was safe, but when we arrived at a café for a light snack, I noticed that the bulge in *The Book of the Angel* was gone. *Oh fuck.* I flipped through the pages—nothing. I looked at my feet, at the ground around them, at the table—no ring. *Shit!*

"I have to go to the bathroom," I blurted then left before she had a chance to respond. As soon as I got to the toilet, I began searching my pockets and, once again, the book. No ring. *What the fuck, you idiot?*

There was nothing I could do. The ring was gone. I didn't leave it in the bedroom where we'd been sleeping. It wasn't in my jacket pocket. It wasn't in *The Book of the Angel.* I'd last seen it during an uphill walk before we entered a shop. Cassandra walked ahead of me a few paces and I took the chance to confirm that the ring was still inside the book. I must've dropped it then. I could go back and look for it, but how would I convince her to walk back with me?

I decided to just propose, to get it over with. If she asked why I had no ring to present, I'd confess the truth. In hindsight, I see what a dumb idea that was. What woman would be happy to hear that her fiancé lost her engagement ring? In all likelihood she'd reject my proposal, which, considering the level of idiocy on the part of the man asking for her hand, would be the smart move.

I rejoined Cassandra.

"You okay?" she asked.

After a few awkward seconds, I said, "No puedo vivir sin tí."

"What?"

I repeated the sentence.

"Why are you speaking to me in your bad Spanish?"

"Did I say it wrong?"

"The pronunciation is terrible."

"Sorry."

"So why are you saying this to me?"

"I… I want to marry you."

I couldn't read her. Normally, she's not one to mask her feelings. I can tell when she's angry, happy, tired. It's never really a mystery with her, but at that moment I had no idea what was going through her head. She undid her poker face and let a smile form slowly.

"Is that what this is for?" she asked then opened her hand, revealing the ring.

"Wait—*how?*"

"In the store. I asked you to hold my camera. You gave me the book for a second. I felt it in there."

"And you took it?"

"I wanted to scare you."

"Mission accomplished."

I was relieved to the extent that I forgot about the lingering unanswered question. At that point, I wasn't sure it mattered. Cassandra, my beautiful imp, delights in fucking with me. Apparently, I make it easy. I was no longer nervous about being rejected (which, come to think of it, would've made for a very awkward flight home). I was just happy to find out that I was less of an idiot than I'd thought.

The tea arrived. It smelled of mint and had some pine nuts floating in it. I drank it down like it was pure alcohol calming my nerves.

Sometime later, as we sat in the café drinking tea and marveling at the beauty of the Mediterranean Sea, Cassandra reminded me that I'd asked her to marry me and, by the way, yes.

"Really?"

"Yes," she said.

"*'Yes I said yes I will Yes.'*"

"What?"

"It's from a book," I said.

"Shut up, already."

Goodbye

December, 2016

My mother is recovering from surgery. The weather is foul, but today I decided that a visit was overdue and driving through snow was the least I could do.

I'd noticed a bit of resistance from her on the phone. She wanted to see me, but she more than implied that she also wanted to rest and not entertain anyone. This is why we skipped Christmas this year. She felt guilty about that, but I told her not to worry. As far as I'm concerned, we can skip it every year.

This rotten year is coming to a close. It's long been my contention that New Year's resolutions are silly. Few of us stick to them, resulting in guilty feelings, and I'm too long past being a practicing Catholic to bother with superficial guilt. But I decided to make a few resolutions anyway because I don't want to live another year like this last one. Here are a few of them:

1. Read more.
2. Write a lot more.
3. Write better.
4. Cook dinner more often.
5. Drink every other day instead of every day.
6. Work harder at being happy.
7. Let the world do its inevitable thing and try to avoid all the horror.
8. Don't ignore the horror to the point of isolation. We're all in it together, fucker.

9. Don't ignore the fact that, despite being a rotten year, I laughed a lot and made a few new friends; that I wrote a few good poems and many bad ones that I might, if I were more motivated, turn into something worthwhile; that I did not starve; that I had a roof over my head; that I am lucky in ways that make my sadness seem foolish; that I'm alive, like it or not, and, despite occasional nihilistic feelings, that's better than not being alive; that any pain I may feel is pretty much the cost of the laughs and the booze and the joy and the poetry and the pizza and the fun; that an unbelievable amount of literature is being published and I can never buy or read it all, so maybe the soft lunacy is a losing game and I'm better off having rid myself of all those dusty tomes last January.

As I was preparing to leave mom's house, she reminded me that I had a few boxes of stuff in her basement that she'd been hanging onto for some time. My stepdad's back was hurting, so she asked if I'd mind getting them out of the basement before he decided to be stubborn and move it all himself.

What did I find in my mom's basement? Boxes of books. Leftovers from 16 years ago when I thought I was moving to Asheville, North Carolina. I was supposed to send her money to ship them to me, but, in all the drama of that stupid venture, I must've forgotten about them. And there they were, waiting this whole time.

"Jesus, look at this," I said. Among the other paperbacks and musty clothbound books was a copy of *The Devil's Dictionary* by Ambrose Bierce. I remember Ralph and I looking it over one night at the bookshop and cracking up at entries like, "Cynic, n. A blackguard whose faulty vision sees things as they are, not as they ought to be," and, "History, n. An account mostly false, of events mostly unimportant, which are brought about by rulers mostly knaves, and soldiers mostly fools." I thumbed through some pages and laughed, the book, sleeping all these years in a box in my mother's basement, alive again in my hands, amusing me again just as it had a decade prior.

I can sell some of my books, but they'll come back. They never go away. They wait years like cicadas, but they're always there. They'll bury me. That's my fate: to be surrounded by books. To die with them. They're my true companions, my obsession, probably my killers. They'll smother me. They'll weigh me down. They'll break my back. They'll obliterate my bank account and ruin my eyes and pester my sinuses. A bent gray creature covered in dust—that's my future. And when they finally do me in, the books will have done so because I dared try to get rid of them. The most vindictive books will be the ones I've not read, which will always be the majority, the heavy books that'll really crack my skull: *War and Peace, Infinite Jest, Gravity's Rainbow.* I'll die in a dimly lit room in some creaky Chicago apartment in winter, pinned down by a fallen tower of hardbacks. Cause of death: The Soft Lunacy.

ABOUT THE AUTHOR

Vincent Francone is the author of the memoir *Like a Dog*. He won 1st place in the 2009 Illinois Emerging Writers Competition, and his work has appeared in *Rain Taxi, Rhino, New City, Three Percent*, and other web and print journals. He teaches composition and hosts a podcast, *Drinking and Talking*.
www.vincentfrancone.com

www.ingramcontent.com/pod-product-compliance
Lightning Source LLC
Chambersburg PA
CBHW051245250626
47155CB00009B/3170